GW00647647

THE HIGH PLACES

THE HIGH PLACES

LEAVES FROM A LAKELAND NOTEBOOK

A. HARRY GRIFFIN

ILLUSTRATIONS BY *AWainwright*

EDITED BY PETER HARDY

F

FRANCES LINCOLN LIMITED
PUBLISHERS

Frances Lincoln Ltd
4 Torriano Mews
Torriano Avenue
London NW5 2RZ
www.franceslincoln.com

Title page: High Stile, from Gatesgarth

CONTENTS

1960s

1970s

INTRODUCTION

This book offers readers a unique opportunity to appreciate a beautiful part of Britain as seen and experienced through the eyes of two masters of their own art; two men who shared a mutual love and passion for the Lake District for most of their lives and until their final days. One was a renowned and well-respected journalist and author of more than a dozen books; the other was a borough treasurer who achieved lasting fame as the creator of an iconic set of seven walking guides.

The text comes from the dedicated work of A.H. Griffin, better known as Harry Griffin, who, while working in Kendal for the *Lancashire Evening Post*, wrote a weekly feature under the title 'Leaves from a Lakeland Notebook'. Three additional pieces, 'The Highest Building?', 'Steep Grass' and 'Eyes of the Mountain', have been selected from an unfinished manuscript that Harry Griffin was working on shortly before his death in 2004. Readers will note that some factual information included in the text may now be out of date, but Harry Griffin's articles have been left as they were originally written. For example, the Post Office Tower is no longer the tallest building in England ('The Highest Building?'), and much of the dense forest in Ennerdale has now been removed ('Magnificence of Pillar Rock'). Also, a scree gully near Pike o' Stickle is now so eroded and slippery that the local Mountain Rescue Association has asked walkers to regard the area as out of bounds, and searching for stone axes is now definitely discouraged ('Pike o' Stickle').

The accompanying illustrations are the work of A. Wainwright, or A.W. to his admirers, and for the most part they have been selected from his five-volume Lakeland Sketchbook series.

Harry Griffin, whose father was a painter and decorator, began in earnest to pursue his interest in outdoor activities, most notably rock climbing, after taking himself on a bicycle ride from his home in Barrow to Coniston as a teenager. After climbing Coniston Old Man, he wandered down the slopes to Goat's Water and saw, for the first time at close quarters, the impressive heights of Dow Crag and then the inspiring sight of climbers bravely scaling the wall of rock, to which they clung with apparent ease and confidence. At that moment he decided that he wanted to do the same.

In 1929, after reading up on rock climbing at Barrow Library, Harry decided that he needed to obtain some expert advice and so presented himself at the offices of George Basterfield, mayor of Barrow and at that time also president of the Fell and Rock Climbing Club. Harry was duly advised where he should go to get his boots nailed properly in preparation for climbing, and, unexpectedly, Mr Basterfield also offered the enthusiastic youth before him the opportunity of some climbing lessons on Dow Crag. Such are the rewards for those who dare to ask, and so started a lifetime of adventures on the mountains, with friends and a number of famous names in the history of Lake District rock climbing.

In the years to come Harry Griffin climbed in the Lake District, Scotland, the Alps, the Himalayas and the Canadian Rockies. In the early 1930s he was one of the founding members of a Lake District climbing club, known as the Coniston Tigers, which established a climbing hut, only the second of its kind, in a converted wooden garage near the shore of Coniston Water.

Harry Griffin's career in journalism began when he was taken on as a trainee by the *Barrow Guardian*. He then moved to the *Lancashire Daily Post*, after which, in 1937, he became a staff reporter with the *Daily Mail* in Manchester. After the war, in which he attained the rank of lieutenant colonel and saw service in Burma under Lord Mountbatten, he was demobilised and briefly returned to his job with the *Daily Mail*. As luck would have it, he heard from an associate that the *Lancashire Evening Post* was looking to expand in the north, offering a new position based at Kendal. He attended the interview dressed impressively in his military uniform and succeeded in obtaining the job. In the spring of 1946 he and his young family moved to the fresh air of Kendal, a country market town within easy reach of the fells and crags of Lakeland.

Combined with the day-to-day task of reporting the local news and eventually becoming Northern Editor, there was a further commitment in his role – a new weekly column was instigated with the title 'Leaves from a Lakeland Notebook'. For almost thirty years

Harry Griffin diligently wrote this regular feature, without a break except for a few short holiday periods. This marathon undertaking was in addition to his record fifty-three-year unbroken series of 'Country Diary' entries for the *Guardian*, from 1951 to just a few days before his death in 2004. After he retired from full-time work in January 1976 Harry Griffin went on to write further regular columns for the *Lancashire Evening Post*. These later features were written under new titles, including 'Mountain High' and 'The View from Harry Griffin'.

At first the 'Leaves' column, written anonymously by Harry under the pen name of 'Dalesman', consisted of several short pieces, which were combined into one article and which might include topics varying from increases in the local rates, the provision of utilities, such as mains electricity to Borrowdale and Langdale, forthcoming social events, such as shepherds' meets or concerts, and the condition of local roads. Before long Harry also began to include notes on his weekend activities, with maybe a few paragraphs recalling a day spent climbing on Gimmer Crag or walking on Coniston Old Man. Sitting for a few moments to enjoy a smoke while drinking in the views was a pleasure he often savoured. In time, the 'Leaves' pieces became more focused on one particular subject or theme each week. Another significant change was that the identity of the writer was revealed – the name A.H. Griffin appeared in print at the head of each piece.

A routine was established every Tuesday at home, when Harry would set himself to work in his study until that week's 'Leaves' piece was completed in readiness for the *Post*'s Friday edition. Sandra Parr, Harry's daughter, remembers that as children she and her brother Robin had to keep very quiet, and preferably far away, as their father became very cross if he were interrupted during his work. The study was his private sanctuary, and he was secretive about his writing. On the few occasions that the two children were summoned into the room, it was for them to be severely reprimanded by their father for some perceived misdemeanour. Sandra remembers that her mother, Mollie, was not even allowed to dust or tidy the room.

A series of scrapbooks was built up over the next three decades. Each week Harry would cut out the 'Leaves' article, which would be retained for future reference. It is from these meticulously collected cuttings that the pieces contained in this book have been selected, from an archive of around 1,500 articles and over one and a half million words, as stated by the author himself in his final 'Leaves' entry.

There were some topics on which Harry Griffin regularly voiced his dissatisfaction over the years. One such subject was the growing problem of tourist traffic on the roads, especially around the Easter holidays. He was also irritated by the number of cairns being built by walkers on the summits of popular fells, making them seem more like obstacles and hindrances than being useful for their originally intended purpose as navigation aids. Harry aired his displeasure on this particular theme for a number of years before guiltily confessing to his readers that he had, in fact, built one himself as a youngster on one of his early fell-top expeditions. The standard of accommodation provided by some of the guest houses and hotels in Lakeland also came in for criticism, as did some of the food served to the new influx of wealthy American tourists – but back in 1948 the mutton pie and tatie-pot served up by Mrs Edmondson, a farmer's wife at Seathwaite, were said to be without equal!

While the council workers who drove the gritting trucks and snow ploughs in the winter months to keep the roads clear of snow and ice often received fulsome praise from Harry, the proposals for a new road over the remote Styhead Pass did not. Neither did the local businessman who came up with a scheme for cable cars over the waters of Windermere and revolving restaurants on the roofs of skyscraper-style hotels to attract more tourists.

But most of all, what is apparent from his writing is that Harry Griffin loved the Lake District with an absolute passion, and this is what comes across when he writes about his days spent out in the mountains, whether clambering on Pillar Rock or walking over Fairfield with Sambo his border collie, skating on Tarn Hows at Christmas or swimming in cool, hidden tarns after a day of rock climbing in the oppressive heat of summer.

Harry Griffin was acquainted with many well-known characters and celebrities in the Lake District, partly as a result of his work as a journalist. He knew Donald Campbell, who was killed on Coniston Water in *Bluebird*. Norman Nicholson the poet and Heaton Cooper the artist were also his friends, as were more eccentric characters, such as Millican Dalton, the Professor of Adventure, and the comical 'Owd Joe', a Wasdale shepherd who spoke in strange tongues. Of course, he also knew Alfred Wainwright, whose illustrations accompany his writings in this book.

Wainwright, from humble beginnings in Blackburn living under the shadows of the cotton mills, achieved unforeseen fame after producing his seven-volume *Pictorial Guide to the Lakeland Fells*, a task to which he committed thirteen years of his life in the evenings and weekends, while also fulfilling his professional duties in the borough treasurer's offices at Kendal Town Hall. A.W. moved to Kendal four and a half years before Harry Griffin and, coinciden-tally, also found work there when the vacancy was mentioned to him by a friend.

Although his name was well known locally and, as each succes-sive *Pictorial Guide* was published, also increasingly familiar among walkers in the Lake District, Wainwright became more widely appreciated after his guides to the Pennine Way and, most especially, his own long-distance route *The Coast to Coast Walk*, which was published in 1973. In partnership with the photogra-pher Derry Brabbs, A.W. produced seven large-format photographic books. The first of these, *Fellwalking with Wainwright*, was published in 1984. It gained Wainwright national recognition when it went rapidly onto the bestseller lists. He was then persuaded to make a series of television programmes with the BBC, with the first of these being filmed in 1985 and seen nation-ally the following year. Wainwright was now a household name, and Kapellan, the animal sanctuary at Grayrigg just outside Kendal, was the beneficiary, since A.W. refused to accept any of the royalties earned on his books, the money instead being used to support Animal Rescue, Cumbria, the charity that ran Kapellan and with which he and his wife Betty were strongly associated.

According to Harry Griffin, the two of them first met around 1948, possibly in A.W.'s office at Kendal Town Hall. For a number of years Wainwright would be seen each weekend, standing at a bus stop on the pavement outside the Griffin family home on Windermere Road in Kendal, waiting to catch a bus to take him off to whichever fell he was currently researching. Harry Griffin recalled that they went walking together on the fells on possibly only two or three occasions.

In 1955 the first volume of Wainwright's *Pictorial Guides, The Eastern Fells*, was published. Harry Griffin wrote a review of the book that confirmed the identity of the author. This was printed in the *Lancashire Evening Post* on 27 May 1955, and the piece is included in this collection. A pattern was established: as each of the six following *Pictorial Guides* was published, so it was reviewed and commented on in the 'Leaves' column.

Few details of the personal association between Harry Griffin and Alfred Wainwright are known, but I think it is reasonable to say that they both greatly respected each other's literary work and achievements. Book Five of Wainwright's *Scottish Mountain Drawings* was dedicated to Harry Griffin who, some years later, made the comment that A.W. might be considered a genius. Furthermore, in recognition of their individual works, they were both awarded the MBE.

Many of the cultural and farming traditions of Cumbria have now been lost or are in decline. Sheep farming is often said to be in crisis, and the prospect of wind-farms littering the landscape is now a regular threat. If we are to believe everything that we now hear on the subject of global warming, it seems likely that future generations will not be able to experience the thrill of skiing down the slopes of a snow-covered Raise or, in the event of droughts, it could be that many of the small mountain tarns will disappear and the joy of a secluded, reviving bathe will become an unknown pleasure.

Perhaps worst of all, Mrs Edmondson's mutton pie can no longer be savoured by tired walkers. But the cairns still seem to multiply!

Despite all these changes, here, in the writing of A.H. Griffin and the illustrations of A. Wainwright, the mountains and fells of Lakeland can still be celebrated and a unique history remembered, and the unfortunate ones, as Harry Griffin refers to them, those who live elsewhere and are unable to see the fells every day of the year, can take pleasure in imagining that they are there, on the summit of Fairfield, Dow Crag or Skiddaw.

ACKNOWLEDGMENTS

Various people provided invaluable assistance over a two-year period, beginning in July of 2005, when the idea for this book was first conceived, and it is only right that the individuals concerned are mentioned and sincerely thanked for their personal contributions.

First, my sincere thanks go to Sandra Parr for allowing the use of Harry Griffin's material and also for patiently exchanging a host of e-mails with me, for answering a thousand and one questions, and for her forthright and considered opinions, which I have appreciated and valued. It has been a pleasure to collaborate with her, and I apologise if I have at times kept her, and her husband Tony, away from the golf courses of Vancouver. I am privileged to have been given the opportunity to work with the writings of Harry Griffin.

I am immensely grateful to the Wainwright Estate for agreeing to allow the drawings by Alfred Wainwright to be used in this book. It is a great privilege to be able to include them, and I would like to thank Betty Wainwright for her permission.

Also, many thanks to Jenny Dereham, who was Alfred Wainwright's editor for many years.

I am extremely grateful to John Nicoll, of Frances Lincoln Ltd, who responded positively when I first contacted him to discuss the idea for this book and also gave me much needed expert guidance and advice at various stages as progress was made.

I also received help from a number of people in Kendal. First, Michael Crossley, a lifelong friend of the Griffin family, who assisted me immensely when I made several journeys north for research purposes. Richard Hall and his colleagues at the Cumbria Record Office in Kendal gave professional and willing service as I read through the archive of Harry Griffin's personal scrapbooks containing his collection of 'Leaves from a Lakeland Notebook' newspaper cuttings (Ref: WDX 1488). Linden Burke of Kirkland Books was also helpful.

Claire Sutton at the Harris Reference Library in Preston also gave important assistance.

On behalf of myself and Sandra Parr, Harry Griffin's daughter, thanks are expressed to the *Lancashire Evening Post*, which gave consent for the 'Leaves from a Lakeland Notebook' articles to be reproduced in book form, and in particular special thanks to Peter Richardson, Features Editor.

I must thank Jayne, my lovely wife, who encouraged and supported me as I pursued this project. Jayne shares my fondness of Lakeland and always sets a good pace for me to keep up with as we haul ourselves up and down the fells.

Peter Hardy

1940s

Gimmer Crag, Great Langdale

GIMMER CRAG
30 May 1947

There's no more pleasant way of spending a summer Sunday afternoon than climbing, in old clothes and well-worn rubber shoes, the clean, sunny face of Gimmer Crag in Langdale and enjoying long smokes in the sunshine between pitches.

That is how I spent last Sunday, one of Lakeland's best days this year, and as I perched, hauling in my second's rope, or sat resting on the summit terrace, I had plenty of opportunity of marvelling – as I had done a hundred times before – at the beauty of the valley beneath and the hills around.

Nearly 2,000 feet below you could see the speck-like sheep, grazing in the patchwork of fields between their old stone walls, here and there the darker brown of newly–ploughed soil, across the valley the old track, climbing over to Blea Tarn, and all around the big blue circle of the Coniston tops, Crinkle Fells and Bowfell. And the only sounds were the rustle of the rope sliding over the edge of the rock, the trickle of some nearby stream and occasionally the cry of a bird or the slipping of scree below the crag.

MILLICAN DALTON
10 October 1947

Hidden in the trees above the lovely pools of the Derwent, underneath the rocks of Castle Crag in Borrowdale, there is a dark cave where, for most of a lifetime, there dwelt one of the most remarkable men in Cumberland.

Earlier this year he died at the age of eighty. I knew him well, and it was almost as a pilgrim that I sought out his cave to see what memories he had left behind. Stuck inside an old teapot along with a few dried dates I found a note from somebody signing himself M.F. Bowser. The note read: 'Hope you are enjoying life as much we used to do. Sorry you were not at home when I called. Thanks for the use of your hearth and cushion.'

Poor old Millican Dalton – that was the name of the recluse – was probably already dead when his friend called. He used to spend a month or so in London each year, and when he left Borrowdale last winter to go south he told an artist friend in the valley: 'I am getting old. I do not think I will ever see Borrowdale again.' And he never did.

Millican Dalton was an educated man who preferred to be close to nature rather than among the busy struggle of modern life. He threw up a job in the City – I think he was a solicitor – and came to live in Borrowdale. There, for very much longer than I can remember, he lived a Robin Hood life – rock climbing, mountaineering, shooting 'rapids', sailing his raft on Derwentwater and always ready to give a hand or hospitality to any wayfarer among the fells.

He looked like Robin Hood too, for he wore a sort of Tyrolese hat with a feather in it, jaunty shorts, mountain boots, a rope over his shoulder and an aggressive Elizabethan beard. His skin was burned brown by sun and exposure. Even at seventy he must have been one of the fittest men in Lakeland.

Millican Dalton's Cave, Borrowdale

Now he is gone, and only his old cave remains to remind one of a happy vagabond. The rusty teapot, a cracked cup and saucer, his cushion, a few old tins and a broken mirror on the rock floor are the only possessions of the old 'Professor of Adventure' left behind in the cave. We may never see his like again.

BOWDER STONE
30 April 1948

I've never been fond of the Bowder Stone, or rather of its associations. The actual stone itself does not offend, but the ladder up its side, the visitors' book and pen at its foot, the picture postcards at the cottage nearby and the tourists who are more interested in its mere bulk than in the magnificent view from the top remind me rather of a Blackpool peepshow. In my view, the less of this sort of thing in Lakeland the better.

The Bowder Stone, Borrowdale

I know there are people who have come by bus or car to be near the Bowder Stone, climbed up the ladder (or, stretched out on the ground, shaken hands with a friend underneath) and then gone back home again, fondly imagining they have seen all there is to be seen in Borrowdale. This is what comes from the wrong sort of publicity.

I am prompted to write thus by the recent sad death of Mr John Pepper of Bowder Stone House, who, with his wife, has been the 'custodian' of the stone for thirty years. How many times he told visitors the size or estimated weight of the stone I would not like to guess.

Probably the Bowder Stone is the biggest isolated boulder in the Lake District, but there are several nearly as big, notably the Pudding Stone near Low Water in the Coniston fells, which has about eight hard rock climbing routes upon it. In fact, there are so many large boulders nearly as big as a house in this little hidden fold in the hills that it is known as Boulder Valley.

Another boulder well known to rock climbers is the Y-Boulder in Mosedale, near Wasdale Head, which has nearly a score of routes up it, one of which can be done feet foremost. Other well-known boulders in Lakeland include the Gash Rock in Langstrath – long reputed to be inaccessible and called after the name of the man who first climbed it – and the Sphinx or Cat Rock on Great Gable (depending on which way you look at it).

Incidentally, I am told that you can see the face of the Scandinavian sun-god Balder on the Bowder Stone (they say this is the derivation of the name). He was supposed to have been killed by an arrow made from mistletoe, and it is said that you can (with the eye of faith) actually see the small hole in the centre of his forehead where the arrow entered.

WIND
7 January 1949

The other day a man was killed in the Lake District by the force of the wind. He was knocked off the back of a lorry by the cover, blown off by a wind that men of the district said was the worst they had ever

The path to Scafell Pike from Esk Hause

known. 'They call it "the wind in the crack",' one quarryman told the Coroner. 'I've known it on the fells, but never before in the valley.' The accident was in the Coniston area, and the sudden gust had whipped like a hurricane through the Yewdale valley from the sea in the south.

There are many places in the Lake District that have reputations for dangerous winds, so much so that this corner of England, shown by statistics to be the wettest part of the country, may also perhaps be the windiest. Most of the valleys have local stories of strange and fierce winds. There is the Helm Wind of Cross Fell, which has tempted the researches of scientists; the sudden squalls that the Windermere boatmen know; the unaccountable Borrowdale wind, which is believed to have led to aircraft disasters; and others.

A man who has been on Everest once told me that the winds that sweep across the great, high plains of Tibet are the worst he has ever known, and I have had experience of the phenomenal gales of Orkney and Shetland. But the worst winds I have ever met have been on top of Esk Hause, that 2,370 foot high pass at the head of a cluster of valleys. At times the gales surge up one or more of these valleys with a force that prevents movement against the wind and blows many people over. I have seen strong men, well used to the hills, reach the shelter on the top – merely two walls built against the wind – in a state of exhaustion because of the gale.

For some reason, probably the funnel effect of the valleys, winds on Esk Hause have appeared stronger than those met with on any summit, although I have been blown over by sudden gusts on mountain tops more than once. And sometimes on the south side of Goat's Water – between Coniston Old Man and Dow Crags – the spray is lifted a hundred feet into the air.

Perhaps one feature of the winds in our hills is that one minute you can be in the centre of what feels like a tornado, and the next, by moving a pace or two, you may be in perfect calm with not even the sound of the wind in your ears. This wind sound, when you are in the middle of it, can be deafening, with the roar as it sweeps up a rock gully or the sharp crack as it breaks against a cliff. Only the great birds, notably the buzzards, seem to be able to battle against our strong winds. The smaller ones are soon driven from the heights.

EEL CRAGS
6 May 1949

It is remarkable, but nevertheless true, that although there are more people climbing rocks and mountains today than there have ever been, it is still possible to find places in the Lake District never reached before and to see completely new views for the first time in history.

I am not referring to the new rock climbs on well-marked crags – although these are still being discovered – but rather to the 'discovery' of completely 'new' crags. Obviously, these crags have been seen by shepherds and walkers, and no doubt sheep have fallen down them and been killed, but some of them are now being explored for the first time, and every foot of ascent has been up completely virgin rock.

The best known recent example of this sort of enterprise has been the discovery of Shepherd's Crag, in Borrowdale, which, until a former Everest mountaineer saw its possibilities, had been noticed only through a belt of trees as a most unlikely looking lump of overhanging precipice. Already it has become one of the most popular climbing grounds, and there are now more than a score of routes up its smooth, steep walls.

Before most climbers have been able to tick off all the new adventures here, there comes news of the new 'discovery' of another crag, several times the size of its Borrowdale forerunner, a discovery that is possibly the biggest in the Lake District of the past twenty years.

The 'new' crag – climbers call their normal haunts 'existing' crags – is the very long one I have always known as Eel Crags, high up on the western slopes of High Spy on the Catbells range and overlooking the lovely vale of Newlands but well above the old Goldscope lead mines. Hundreds of walkers pass along this ridge in the summer, and thousands must have noticed the crag from the summit of Dale Head,

Eel Crags, Newlands

but until some West Cumberland and Keswick climbers began exploring recently nobody had ever been there before. The crags have always looked either too rotten, too easy or just impossible.

Now the pioneers have found them to consist of perfect rock with chances of dozens of new long, steep, natural routes and the work of exploration is going ahead.

QUARRYMEN'S HUTS
13 May 1949

On the way up the old Rigghead Quarries track from Borrowdale into Newlands for my promised visit to Eel Crags, I noticed again the remains of the quarrymen's and miners' huts and marvelled at the sort of men they must have been. The huts – rough, single–roomed places – were perched on this very steep track between 1,000 and 1,500 feet above the valley floor, and the men used to live up there several days at a time. The huts have all tumbled in now, but you can still see how the inside walls were whitewashed and where the men used to light their fires. You would not get miners to live and work under those conditions today.

From Eel Crags you can see little of the way the Newlands valley has been churned up with mines and quarries during the last few hundred years. Most of the old spoil heaps have now grown over and become part of the countryside, but when you get down into the valley you can see the shafts, tunnels, water cuttings and old foundations, which are all that are left of the industrialisation of the past.

A few hundred years ago this area was an important centre of lead, copper, silver and gold mining, and it is said that most of the timber of Lakeland was cut down in order to provide the miners with charcoal to smelt their ore.

The remains of many of the old paths used by the miners of centuries ago can still be seen, but there were two paths that puzzled me. They led from the neighbourhood of the old Goldscope lead mines to a point somewhere beneath the summit of Dale Head and then petered out at a height of about 2,000 feet. There was no

The head of Newlands

Birks Bridge, Duddon Valley

mining up there, and there were no signs of quarrying either, but the paths have been used by sledges.

I wonder whether these old 'sledgates' have any connection with the more famous Moses' Sledgate across the back of Gable to Honister. 'Moses' has often been credited with being a whisky smuggler, but perhaps it was plumbago, or even gold from Newlands, that he stored in a hidden cache under Dale Head!

PERFECT BATHING
1 July 1949

The music of Lakeland – the merry sound of its tumbling becks and foaming gills and the tinkle of a thousand tiny streamlets lapping against the boulders and dancing in the sunlight – has been remarkably stilled during the last few weeks of cloudless skies. A strange quiet has crept over the dales.

Hundreds of becks have disappeared, waterfalls have dried up, and even the lovely Derwent, born in the mountains above Seathwaite, England's wettest corner, has become, in places, just a shy trickle among the littered rocks and stones. But fortunately, there have always been plenty of opportunities for bathing in Lakeland – superb bathing of a type not found elsewhere in the country – if you know where to look for it.

Some people like to bathe in the sea breakers off the west Cumberland coast, others prefer the fun of a day at Grange open-air swimming pool, while many enjoy diving from a boat into one of the larger lakes, but I am referring particularly to bathing in the high tarns or in the scores of beautiful pools, which, like glistening pearls, adorn many of our mountains' becks.

Last Sunday evening I bathed in Goat's Water, 1,646 feet above sea level, in the high corrie west of Coniston Old Man. The sun had left the tarn an hour before, the last climber had come down off the buttresses of Dow Crag and trotted down to the valley, and the only people about were two men trying to tempt reluctant trout with home-tied flies. The only sounds were the lazy rising of the fish and the bleat of a lamb seeking its mother on the rocky slopes above.

It was, like dozens in the same place before it, a perfect bathe, but there are many better spots in Lakeland where you may refresh tired limbs and recapture the exhilaration that weather such as we have been having recently tends to destroy. The best places are pools, and the finest are those of the upper Esk, Langstrath and perhaps the Duddon.

To bathe at the end of a hot, tiring day in the clear depths of one of those rock-girt caverns, where every pebble, yards down, is perfectly visible, is an experience no artificial pool can provide.

Blackmer Pot, in Langstrath, must be one of the deepest and most remarkable pools in Lakeland. You can dive from almost any height you care to choose and never touch the bottom and yet never be more than a yard or two from the side, and you can swim in safety among wonderful rock scenery. Birks Bridge on the Duddon has its fine pool; there is another one at the foot of Stanley Ghyll Force in Eskdale; a third in Church Beck above Coniston; several, fringed with trees, in Borrowdale; yet another near the foot of Scarth Gap; tiny ones in Mickleden and under Skiddaw, and – oh, scores and scores of them.

You don't need a towel for this sort of bathing, or so I was once told by a German scientist. You pull your clothes onto your wet body. It's easy if you are really wet. The water goes back into your pores – or something like that – and it does you a great deal of good.

I do not claim – as the scientist did – that you can cure all sorts of ailments by this method, but it has its conveniences.

OWD JOE OF WASDALE HEAD
30 September 1949

When I knew, twenty years ago, that delightful, red-bearded old fellow, 'Owd Joe' of Wasdale Head, who knew more about sheep and less about anything else than almost anybody I have ever known, I was often told the tale of the only time he ever left the dale.

The story was designed to prove that, although 'Owd Joe' had never seen a bus or a train or a lamppost, he was not so simple as he looked. I think it was Egremont where they sent him, the occasion,

Wasdale Head

I believe, being a fair. They packed him off in the car or trap and gave him a shilling, and away went Joe with a wicked grin across his toothless face. Late that night he returned, drunk as a lord, with a look of supreme satisfaction below his tousled head – and two shillings in his pocket.

But there was an embellishment to the story. In addition to his alcoholic incoherency, complicated by the fact that he had no teeth, Joe was also unintelligible for another reason – he was mouthing a foreign language. And the language, it was said, was Icelandic.

They brought professors and scholars staying at the hotel to listen to his ramblings, and they all agreed – it definitely sounded Scandinavian.

Now, I am not going to attempt to explain the story, although the temptation to write of a mysterious link still remaining between the Vikings of a thousand years ago and this untutored shepherd of a west Cumberland dale is strong. After all, 'Owd Joe' counted his sheep by a set of outlandish numerals that are said to have come down from the earliest British tribes who lived in Cumberland long before the Norsemen came.

But it is really remarkable the number of Cumberland and Westmorland folk who have never realised that they might be descendants of Vikings.

ON BOWFELL
16 December 1949

The most fortunate people in the Lake District last Sunday – in my view – were the very few who were out on the top of the mountains. Certainly Sunday was a day in a thousand and in sharp contrast to much of the rest of this week with its teeming rain and chilling winds.

Two of us were on the top of Bowfell, on our way back from Great End, where we had hoped to find sport with ice axes in the gullies but had been disappointed. We were rewarded, instead, with one of the most remarkable views Lakeland can ever provide and perhaps the finest sunset of the year. The whole of Lakeland, white

Bowfell, from Pike o' Blisco

with new snow, lay stretched out below us, the sun shone down out of a bright blue sky, and the well-known distances seemed to have shrunk overnight.

We felt we could almost throw a stone against the black Scafell crags, 2 miles away across the splendid wilderness of upper Eskdale, while the smoking chimneys of Millom and the brown plantations under Skiddaw seemed only short walks away. The former seaplane hangar on the shore of Windermere looked like an oblong parcel dumped at our feet.

But it was perhaps the really distant views that most interested us. Flat-topped Ingleborough and the other Yorkshire giants were very clear, Criffel in the Scottish lowlands was easily recognisable through the gap between Skiddaw and the Derwent fells, and beyond, apparently hanging from the clouds above the very farthest horizon, were some of the big Scottish mountains, looking like a great Himalayan range.

Haze over the sea and the Lakeland fells themselves prevented a view of the Isle of Man or of distant Ireland, which I have seen from the Lake District on several occasions.

Once at seven o'clock in the morning, after an all-night camp on the top of Scafell, I saw England, Scotland, Ireland and Wales by walking about 100 yards. The first three countries could be seen from where I stood near the top of Deep Ghyll, and by moving a short distance along the summit I could see, reasonably clearly, the Glyder Mountains in North Wales.

Ireland can sometimes be seen from Walney Island, and a friend of mine once saw the Dublin and Wicklow Mountains from the main road above Whitehaven. At the same time he could see the sea all around the Isle of Anglesey and, quite clearly, the North Wales mountains. This, he tells me, was about 11 o'clock in the morning on a showery July day. My Scafell view was, I think, in August.

Sunday's remarkable view was interesting in other ways. For instance, it showed that the eastern half of the district had had more snow than the western (it was fit for skiing on the Helvellyn range) and that Hobcarton Pike and Blencathra, under snow, are among the shapeliest mountains in the district. On Sunday they looked almost Alpine, for there had just been sufficient snow to outline and sharpen their ridges.

Many people consider that the view from High Raise, just across the upper Langdale valley and probably the central point of Lakeland, is the district's finest, but I have always preferred Bowfell, with its rather nearer view of the highest mountains.

The sun was setting like a glorious hanging curtain of gold as we crunched across the frozen surfaces of Three Tarns and along the splintered tops of Crinkle Crags on our way home. Just before it sank out of sight behind Wasdale we saw the afterglow caught on the rocky turrets of the Langdale Pikes, making these modest fells soar like Dolomite spires lit by summer lightning.

It was almost dark as we plunged through the soft snow to the valley, up to the knees in the tracks left by the sheep brought down from the high snows a few hours earlier.

1950s

Langdale Pikes, from Lingmoor Fell

SEARCHING FOR LOST WALKERS
6 April 1951

Searching for lost walkers on the Lakeland fells can be a very depressing and tiring business, but, provided one's own relatives or friends are not involved even mountain searches can have their compensations. For instance, if we had not been out on the tops last Sunday we would have missed, between the snow showers, some of the most magnificent views of the winter as well as that firm comradeship that seemed to pervade the whole of central Lakeland on that day. It was assumed that everybody one met on the fells was engaged in the same task, and it was always pleasant to compare notes. There were many lessons, too, to be learned from Sunday's mass search.

We had our first surprise view when ploughing up the slopes of Pike o' Stickle from the top of the Stake Pass. Since leaving the foot of the pass we had been trudging through deep snow in falling snow and mist, which reduced visibility to a few yards, when suddenly a patch of blue sky appeared through the first cloud gap of the day, and we sat down to watch the transformation.

The first peaks to be unveiled were the many hummocks of Glaramara, looking quite Alpine in their mantle of snow, and then the mist soared away in a great sweep to reveal the distant crags of Great End and the summit of Esk Hause, so thickly plastered in snow that it looked like the Greenland ice cap.

The second view was revealed after a particularly heavy snow blizzard, when we were near the summit of High Raise, which is considered by many people to be the central peak of the Lake District, if you can call this uninteresting, plateau-like summit a peak. From this remote viewpoint, 2,500 feet up, we had an excellent view of Great Gable before the clouds and the snow came down again.

But it was the third view that was easily the most impressive. We had arranged a rendezvous with two other parties on the craggy summit of Pavey Ark and had reached our last 'top' after steering a compass course through the snow and mist. The other parties had been following a possible clue and were late in arriving at the rendezvous, so that we were shivering when the sky suddenly opened up.

I think we all forgot the cold in our admiration of the glorious view. From our feet the black crags of Pavey Ark dropped clear to Stickle Tarn, and just across the column to the south the upper rocks of Harrison Stickle seemed to plunge much more steeply than ever they do in summertime towards the valley. Langdale looked a glorious blaze of colour, with the beck wandering quietly down to Elterwater and the Brathay, and, as a backcloth, there were the tops of Wetherlam, Grey Friar and Carrs, their high snows shining in the sunlight and making them appear ten times their actual height.

The only ones unaffected by the view were two sheep, quietly burrowing through the snow for the few blades of grass that carry on an exposed existence on the very edge of the Pavey Ark precipice. When we were down at the tarn perhaps an hour later we could still see the two sheep silhouetted like black dots against the sky. Why they chose to graze on this particular spot I cannot say. It looked as if a breeze would blow them over the edge.

DALE HEAD
28 March 1952

Returning by an unorthodox route from west Cumberland early one recent evening, I stopped the car on the top of Honister Pass and strolled up towards the clouds to renew a long-standing acquaintanceship with the summit of Dale Head.

It is perhaps a year or two since I was last up there, and I must have forgotten something of the sudden splendour of the view as you reach the cairn. At all events, it so impressed me that I thought it worth while today to pose once again the ancient query, 'Which is the best view in Lakeland?' and put forward a claim for the view from the summit of Dale Head to be included in any shortlist.

The view I am referring to is that to the north – ignoring for a moment the much more massive picture of the highest hills in the Lake District immediately behind you – and probably much of its charm lies in the fact that you see it quite suddenly, without any warning. One moment you are treading the rather dull final slope to the north with

The summit of Dale Head

nothing much to look at in front of you; the next moment the ground suddenly drops away, the great Derwent fells with old man Skiddaw at the back rise up to greet you, and the whole of the lovely vale of Newlands lies smiling in the sunshine 2,000 feet below your feet.

Six miles away the sun glints on the rooftops of Keswick, looking like a toy village under the painted backcloth of Skiddaw, and far beyond the furthest Lakeland fells you can pick out the Scottish hills. One end of Bassenthwaite Lake can just be seen beyond the Lorton Fells, but the glories of Borrowdale are hidden behind the ramparts of Maiden Moor and Eel Crags.

Directly in front of you, if the sun is favourable, the long ridge leading to the summit of Grasmoor stands up vertical and sharp like a piece of stage scenery. The slopes of Causey Pike, Sail, Wandope and the rest appear quite vertical, and the ridge itself, which is a reasonably pleasant but insect-ridden walk in summer, appears almost like a line of Alpine towers. Grisedale Pike peeps up behind this ridge, and to your left the fells sweep round to the twin buttresses of Hindscarth and Robinson.

But it is the view immediately at your feet that always attracts me. From near the cairn the ground appears to drop vertically down the contours of Newlands Beck, which flows due north through a green trough scooped out with perfect symmetry.

You could not wish for a more perfect pastoral scene, but three or four hundred years ago this valley housed an important industry, for the German miners were hard at work, tearing the minerals out of the ground. From some of the new climbs on Eel Crags you can trace where some of these old workings used to run, but on the ground there is little evidence of the work that used to go on in this lovely dale. The map indicates disused lead mines, but there were also copper smelting works in the valley, and it is said that the Goldscope mine has produced both gold and silver.

Long before the coming of the Romans the tribes probably dug for copper in this valley, and it was probably the Romans who discovered the lead and the silver here as well as at the Greenside mines above Glenridding.

In the fourteenth century the lead and silver mines at Alston were managed by a German, and 200 years later the German miners began to settle in Keswick. For a time they were distrusted, and some of them, to be safe, lived on the Derwentwater islands, but they brought prosperity to Keswick, and their anglicised names can still be found in the district. But although these Germans made a great impact on the life and prosperity of Cumberland and Westmorland, their sheds, waterwheels, crushing plants, furnaces and rubbish tips have now more or less disappeared, which is very much more than can be said for other evidences of discarded industry scattered about the Lake District fells.

Apropos of this, I notice that an investigation is going to be made into the methods by which slate quarry dumps and spoil heaps can be covered by vegetation. I know an attempt to do something of this kind has been made at the Greenside lead mines, but it is a very slow and expensive business, and it is difficult to see how anybody could possibly tackle the problem of, for instance, making Coniston Old Man into a mountain again.

Turning your back on the view I will always admire, you have in the foreground the scarred face of Honister Crag on Fleetwith, which is not now worked for slate. Somehow or another, this massive piece of artificial mountainside, which has been blasted and torn until it stands quite vertical in places, has never offended me, and I look kindly upon the quarry huts on top of the pass where the men still work the slate that is won nowadays from the side of Dale Head. The stone is blasted from high up on the mountain and brought in buckets down a precipitous incline and then by a tiny railway down the fellside and across the bridge over the steepest section of the pass and into the quarry sheds for handling by electric saws and the men's chisels.

In the southward view from Dale Head the other evening you could see that Scafell Pike, the highest land in England, is carrying more snow on its northern face than any other mountain. Patches of it may remain there until the summer. Pillar, Great Gable and Scafell Crags seemed almost clear of snow, but there is still some remaining on the north side of the Helvellyn range. The other day there was even a crevasse, several feet deep, on the summit of Sticks Pass.

Comparatively few people bother to go to the top of Dale Head, which is strange since it must be probably the easiest mountain in the Lake District to ascend – if you drive to the summit of Honister. I cannot remember ever seeing anybody on the top, although you can go up and down in an hour. My small boy once ran down from the top to the pass in a very few minutes. Perhaps the most difficult part of this very simple expedition is the drive to Honister summit. I think the last part of the ascent from the Buttermere side must be the steepest bit of main road in Lakeland, but even so it is surprising the number of old cars that can manage it. The old road down the Borrowdale side is still occasionally used by walkers but, by comparison with the smooth motorway, it is beginning to look even rougher than it did when it was the only road.

One wonders when the misplaced suggestion for running bus services over Honister will be revived.

PIKE O' STICKLE
18 July 1952

For something like 4,000 years the neatly chipped stone axe head, which now adorns the fireplace in my study, lay unnoticed among the screes of Pike o' Stickle, the conical-shaped peak overlooking the upper part of the Great Langdale valley. When I picked it up I felt I had taken a long stride back into the days before history began.

Experts assure me that it is a genuine stone axe from the nearby 'factory' 2,000 feet above the valley but that it had been rejected as unsuitable for export because of some inferior chipping at one side. I can imagine that hairy, prehistoric workman, of an age so long ago that our minds cannot bridge the passing centuries, scowling at his 'foreman' when told the axe was no good and hurling his rejected work on a heap of others in a corner.

During the 4,000 years the axe head has slithered only a short distance down the scree, and the stone appears to be in the same condition as when it was thrown down. There is no sign of weathering, and every chipping made by that naked craftsman of long ago is perfectly plain.

The axe is about 8½ inches long and varies in width from about 3½ inches to 2 inches. It is pointed at one end and rounded at the other, and one of the unfinished edges is even now so sharp that I can chop wood with it. The stone is a lovely greenish-grey.

There was nothing remarkable in my find, for a friend of mine has discovered about a dozen Stone Age weapons and tools in the same area. He has even discovered what might turn out to be another 'factory' site in the Lakeland hills, but I must not reveal where this is.

Most of the axes seem to have been found in the screes to the east side of Pike o' Stickle in the area of a band of rock about 2,000 feet above sea level. Antiquarians have discovered a small platform, now well covered with bilberries, and it seems quite likely from the chippings scattered around that the Stone Age workmen fashioned their axes and tools on the boulders at this spot. Other 'workings' have also been discovered nearer the top of Stake Pass, and axes have been found on the path leading from Dungeon Ghyll to Harrison Stickle.

Pike o' Stickle

It has been suggested that other axe factory sites may still be awaiting discovery in Lakeland, and it is even reported that an unfinished axe head was picked up before the recent war high up near the path leading to Scafell Pike. Some antiquarians have wondered whether a small cave in the crags of the gully on the east side of Pike o' Stickle had anything to do with what was probably the first industry in Lakeland, for two partly made-up axes were picked up from the floor. Apparently, however, although the cave is certainly manmade, there is little evidence to connect it with the 'factory'.

For one thing, many of the axes have been picked up higher up the mountainside than the cave. There seem to have been several working sites in the area, and stone implements, besides blocks of stone that might have been used as anvils, have been found close to Gimmer Crag, which is heavily populated with rock climbers on most fine weekends.

According to a recent issue of the *Transactions of the Cumberland and Westmorland Antiquarian and Archaeological Society*, more than 130 roughed-out axes have been found, but I am sure that this total has now been greatly exceeded, for besides my friend's energetic discoveries, there have, I believe, been several finds by other experts. The experts believe that the stone implements made high up in the Langdale Pikes must have left the 'factory' in an unfinished state and been taken outside of the valley for grinding and polishing.

The men probably worked on the mountainside during the spring and summer and then, perhaps, finished off the implements in sheltered huts, probably many miles away, during the winter months.

Axes in many parts of Cumberland, Westmorland and north Lancashire have been identified as likely to have come from the Great Langdale 'factory', and it is suggested that the Stone Age men carried them over the passes, including Ore Gap and Three Tarns, to do the winter finishing.

When the axes were finished they travelled far, and perhaps the Stone Age men were not so parochial as some of us might have thought. Axes that archaeologists state very probably came from

Westmorland have been found in the Isle of Man, in Scotland and in many parts of England, and it is thought that many of the more distant journeys were accomplished largely by boat.

A very fine unpolished axe picked up on Morecambe Golf Course and now in Lancaster Museum is stated almost certainly to have been made in Great Langdale.

WATERFALLS
15 August 1952

There is only one good thing to be said for the wild, wet weather we have been having recently and that is that when it is all over you can see the Lake District in one of its most impressive and exciting moods. Climb up the miserable little trickle of Lodore Falls on many a score of summer days and you may wonder why the poets get so excited about it, but see Lodore this week and you will understand their enthusiasm.

It is a fine sight to see a tremendous volume of water falling sheer for 90 feet between vertical rock walls with a roar that nearly deafens you, and now is the time to watch our Lakeland falls. None of them are tremendously high – Scale Force above Crummock Water with a drop of about 125 feet is the biggest – but even the smaller ones, such as the falls at Throstle Garth in upper Eskdale or Colwith Force, give you a quick insight into nature's extraordinary power and beauty.

John Ruskin thought Dungeon Ghyll Force one of the most magnificent sights he had ever seen – and he had visited Switzerland and other European countries – but perhaps he was exaggerating a little, for there are several Lakeland falls, including Stock Gill near Ambleside, Dalegarth Force near Boot, the well-known Aira Force in Patterdale and the falls of Tilberthwaite Gill near Coniston, that are just as impressive.

Two or three weeks ago, before the really heavy rains, Cam Spout waterfall on the southeastern spur of Scafell was a crashing torrent full of a particularly wild beauty because of its setting among the

Scale Force

highest mountains in England, and this week it must have been a sight worth travelling many miles to see. Then there are the dozens of falls you never hear mentioned, such as that fine trinity that tumble down into Oxendale, Browney Gill, Crinkle Gill and Hell Gill, where there are foaming cascades of 150 feet and more.

The weight of water in these wild ravines would crush the life out of most living things, but if you go to the right places at the right time you may see fish miraculously leaping the smaller falls and making their way upstream against the driving waters. The other day I watched the fish leaping at Force Falls near Kendal, sometimes missing the jump and being hurled back into the boiling pool, other times falling flat on the curling torrent and then forcing their way, with a wriggle of powerful fins, into the quieter water beyond. Sometimes you may see autumn salmon of up to 20 pounds racing up from the salt water and jumping up towards the upper reaches at this point.

But however exciting this river scenery may be just now when the waters are in spate, my personal preference is for the becks and pools of Lakeland when the floodwaters have subsided a little and the streams, nicely filled but quieter, take on their former colours again. Spend a day by one of those foaming becks just now and your ears will be closed to every other sound except the roar and the crash of the brown racing waters, while the dominating colour will be the white of the spray and the churning foam.

But shortly, in the sunny August or September days to come, when the willows change to red and white and the pale gold leaves of the birches begin to flutter down, you will see and hear these secluded Lakeland waters when they can be enjoyed throughout a long autumn day. A sunny September day exploring the pools of the upper Esk or Langstrath or even those of the Duddon or the Derwent can be your most colourful and rewarding Lakeland experience of the year.

A picture in this year's Lake Artists Society exhibition at Grasmere by W. Heaton Cooper shows this colouring to perfection and illustrates the inviting charm of one of these pools. Although the title does not say so, it is easy to see that the pool is Blackmer Pot, the deepest in Langstrath and one of the best places to be in on a really hot day. There are corners of this pool that the sun never reaches, and in the dark vertical walls grow mosses, lichens and shy mountain flowers. In places the gorge through which the pool flows is so narrow that you can leap across, but the water is so deep that even on the stillest day, with not a ripple on the surface, you cannot see the bottom.

Before you jump in for your swim – and there could be no better bathing place – you can watch the water take on every colour imaginable, and the artist has caught this colouring so accurately that just to look at the picture makes you feel cooler. He sat by the pool on many occasions trying to make the water on his canvas appear real, and he has succeeded by painting the deepest part with a green so dark it is almost black.

ON MOSES' TROD
31 October 1952

The clouds racing across the morning sky looked too high for rain, but it was blowing very hard from the west as we drove through Keswick. Obviously we would be blown off the crags unless we chose one with its back to the wind. Finally we agreed on Boat Howe Crags on Kirk Fell and turned the car into Borrowdale, towards the lovely, lazy Derwent and the bonniest birches in Cumberland. There was no sunshine, but the woods around Castle Crag were a blaze of colour. A thick blanket of mist was down to about 2,000 feet on the higher tops.

On the way up the steep track from the quarries where we left the car to the ruined remains of the former Drum House we caught up with an unusual pedestrian – a man carrying a piece of heavy iron piping about 20 feet long. Every time a gust of wind came he was in danger of being spun around and tumbled down the fellside. The piping, he explained, was for a climbing hut that is being established among the fells, the latest addition to the dozen or more of such huts now scattered about the Lake District.

We gave him a lift with the pipe, and he told us that the hut, set above the 1,500 foot contour, has sleeping bunks for twelve men and a view from the front door (the only one) that must be unequalled from a Lake District residence, however temporary.

We were now stepping along the well-known Moses' Trod Sledgate, which winds among the fells from Wasdale, up to Beck Head between Kirk Fell and Great Gable and thence along the shoulders of Brandreth and Grey Knotts to Honister. It is said that Moses was a smuggler and whisky distiller and that this was the track the old smugglers used to and from the sea. Drawings made about a hundred years ago show laden packhorses going along this route, and there is no doubt that it is a very fine track, keeping its height all the way and skilfully avoiding steep drops or ascents. What the connection, if any, there was between Moses' Trod and the Smugglers' Hut on Gable Crag I have never been able to establish with certainty. The 'hut' is a tiny ruined stone building on a sloping grass terrace high up on Gable Crag and inaccessible to the ordinary walker.

Great Gable, from Moses' Trod

If Moses used this cache for storing his whisky he must have been a very tough old bird, and it is difficult to understand why he should have chosen such a place. Another theory is that the building was used by quarrymen to hide wadd, stolen from the former plumbago mine in Borrowdale.

Moses and his confederates would not notice the view, for they would mostly be travelling by night and the beauty of high places had not then been generally discovered, but we found it exhilarating – as always. First, there was the lovely sight of Buttermere and Crummock Water, nestling at the feet of the ring of great fells, with one patch of sunlight catching the summit of Robinson and another glinting on the tiny tarns hidden among the hummocks on the rugged plateau of Haystacks.

Then, ten minutes later, we were looking down the long, straight 7 miles of Ennerdale, with the Liza winding through the forestry plantations, Pillar Rock just showing through the mist and, straight ahead, the arched back of Great Gable with the clouds weaving about the crags.

Ennerdale has changed a great deal in recent years, and the long treeless glen I knew as a boy is no more. Now the whole upper valley is dark with foreign conifers, and its mystery and strange seclusion have gone forever. The woods finish abruptly on the fellside, their boundaries harsh and knife-sharp, and the Liza is disappearing among the growing firs. Seen from this height, the conifers made a bizarre pattern, but the ragged patches on the great sprawling carpet where the rock outcrops have beaten the trees gave the picture a certain amount of crude character. We decided that if the edges of the forest had been treated with a little more imagination the effect would not be disastrous but merely unfortunate.

We reached the scree under Gable Crag, identified the climbs and the position of the Smugglers' Hut and trudged up to Beck Head. Then, picking our way across the boulders on the side of Kirk Fell, we reached the foot of our climbs on Boat Howe.

This climbing ground was first pioneered in 1925 by Professor T. Graham Brown, a well-known Alpine climber, and George Basterfield, the Barrow climber who taught so many people to love the hills, but it was first 'discovered' exactly forty years ago by the first named, who was struck by the impressive shape of the crags. There are now about a dozen climbs on these precipices, all of them with nautical names, for the crags take their name from Boat Howe, the shepherds' name for the knoll that lies below. There are Sea Wall Arete, Starboard Chimney, Hatchway and Rigging, Breakwater Slabs and so on, while the very severe route up the central pillar is called the Prow of the Boat.

When the pioneers named these climbs they imagined the central buttress as a boat lying in harbour with its bows pointing in, and the resulting terminology is among the happiest collections of names out of the many hundreds of Lake District rock climbs.

We spent the afternoon on two of these climbs and then wandered onto the vast summit of Kirk Fell, in its way one of the most massive and least known mountains in the Lake District. Before we turned for home the mists lifted for a few short minutes and there, 10 miles or so away, we saw the sea. It was a most impressive view. Far below us we could see the whitewashed farm and hotel at Wasdale Head, the stone walls around the tiny fields and the twin becks flowing down to Wastwater. The sun was shining on the lake, but the mist hung along the tops of The Screes and blanketed the Pillar Fells.

From here the clouds looked black, and they hung like a sinister curtain right across the westward view, but below the angry clouds the lake waters flashed and sparkled, and far beyond we could see the sunlit meadows and the woods leading down to the coast, and then, as we watched the setting sun dipped slowly towards the sea.

CASTLE ROCK OF TRIERMAIN
18 September 1953

The remarkable way in which native trees can find root and grow in the most unlikely places in the Lake District has always fascinated me. It is not in the least uncommon to see them growing out of solid rock, apparently remote from even a handful of soil, yet carefully

Castle Rock, Legburthwaite

tended 'foreign' trees sometimes fail to live through the first winter after they are planted.

It is, of course, the assorted luxuriance of its tree life that gives Lakeland so much of its great beauty and provides its principal feature of dissimilarity with, say, the mountain area of North Wales. Perhaps there is some association between the arboreal fertility of the Lake District and the decision of the Forestry Commission to experiment with tree improvement by grafting in their new seed orchards at Grizedale, near Hawkshead.

Frequently, one can see native trees growing not only out of solid rock but out of vertical rock, and there are several examples of this sort of remarkable growth in quarries around the Little Langdale area. Last Sunday two of us were climbing on the Castle Rock of Triermain, just off the Stanah to Threlkeld road, and we saw many instances of oak, mountain ash, birch and even yew trees sprouting sturdily through the rock. Much of this impressive crag is vertical, and in parts it is overhanging, but the trees seem to have no difficulty in flourishing without visible soil and with nothing but fresh air above and below.

There are not a great number of yew trees in the Lake District, and the stranger might well spend a day touring the area and not see one, but there are any number growing in this remarkable vertical 'forest'.

It is rather strange that such a prominent Lake District feature close to a main road should be more or less ignored in the popular guidebooks   a fact appreciated by climbers since it enables them to operate unwatched by the crowds of motorists that nowadays embarrass performers on the lower crags in upper Langdale every Sunday. The Castle Rock is in the Vale of St John's, and from the top of it you look down on the traffic speeding along the Ambleside to Keswick road, but the motorists are too far away to notice the tiny figures on the crag.

Sir Walter Scott, in his *The Bridal of Triermain*, made some reference to the rock appearing like a castle, and this is no doubt how the crag came by its romantic-sounding name. Other early writers referred to the crag as a castle, and it is true that even today there are the remains of some ancient building that might have been a fort on the top. So far as I know nobody has ever been able to tell us much about this building. The late Professor W.G. Collingwood thought that it might have been built by a descendant of the Vikings before the coming of the Normans.

It is said that the Vale of St John's derives its name from the Knights Hospitallers of St John, for the little church on the hill between this valley and the River Naddle once belonged to this sect. The crag itself was first 'discovered' for climbing purposes by a Liverpool doctor, and the modern fierce routes up the overhangs were first led by a well-known Lake District climber.

WILDLIFE
1 January 1954

One of the delights of getting about on the fells throughout the year is the chance of seeing the wildlife of the district and, occasionally, of watching creatures that are unaware of your presence. To see a fox sunning himself on a rock or taking a quiet stroll across his own land is a far more rewarding spectacle than watching him run for his life. The sight of a flock of whooper swans spreading their wings and trumpeting with excitement as they come in to land on perhaps Elterwater or Little Langdale Tarn can brighten many a dull December day.

Looking through my diary of one year on the fells I am reminded of many encounters with wild creatures and of several lovely, almost intimate, sights. One of the loveliest pictures you can get in the fells is the sight of wild geese, flying homeward against an evening sky, with the hills turning purple in the sunset and perhaps the first lights beginning to flicker in the valley. The last time I saw this picture was near the summit of Harter Fell, in Westmorland, at the close of a winter's day, with snow on the ground, the moon just beginning to come up and visibility stretching for miles. The geese – greylags, I think they were – came over in V-shaped formation, their long necks extended, their greyish-brown plumage easily recognisable, and every

Elterwater

now and then they honked out their characteristic croak. Just after flying directly overhead, the leader changed his course by about 10 degrees – just as if he was making a compass correction – and the gaggle continued on its new course, a perfect piece of formation flying. They were probably flying from Morecambe Bay to the Solway, and I can remember they made a fine romantic sight.

In many recent winters whooper swans have been about in fairly large numbers, and each year scores of them fly down from the frozen north to winter on our tarns. The biggest flock I have seen was about thirty on Derwentwater. The notes of these big birds sound just like bugle calls, and when they are quietly feeding you can hear them making a peculiar low, musical song. The principal difference in appearance between the whooper swan and the ordinary mute swan seen on rivers and ponds is that the wilder bird has a yellow and black bill – yellow at the base – while the other has the colours roughly reversed or, more correctly, black and orange.

During every year I see nearly all the birds of the fells – ravens, buzzards, kestrels, peregrines and so on. I can remember spending about an hour one morning watching with binoculars a peregrine, a study in grey and white, quietly sitting high in a steep crag in a very remote valley. I like to think he was unaware of our presence, but I am not sure about this. This very fierce falcon is by no means extinct in our district, although many people would have you believe so. Probably he is the sworn enemy of the pigeon fanciers, whose birds fly up and down certain Lake District valleys.

One of the most interesting birds I saw one year was a rough-legged buzzard, a larger bird than the common type, and the nearest approach to an eagle you will get in this country. I saw him gliding silently over Pasture Rock above Low Hartsop and for a moment thought he must be an eagle. He was very close indeed and either had not seen me or was not greatly worried, for he took his time to fly very slowly to a tree on the opposite side of the beck and then sat there until it grew dark. His thick-feathered legs were very plain indeed, and he was not so dark in colour as the ordinary buzzard, with quite a lot of whitish colour about his underparts.

Several times I have been lucky enough to see a fox before it saw me, and on at least one occasion when he never saw me at all. This occasion was on Dow Crag near Coniston. The Coniston Foxhounds were out in the district, and we had heard them somewhere back of the Old Man. I was bringing a man up a chimney and looking straight down onto the screes when I saw a fox slowly picking its way across the foot of the gully. When he reached the boulders below us he stopped, looked around him and then slowly plodded on. A second two later – would you believe it? – a second fox also crossed the foot of the gully and slowly disappeared. The hounds were nowhere in sight, and for all I know these two were not being hunted. Before the day was out the hunt had killed a fox, but whether it was one of the two we had seen I cannot say.

On another occasion I watched a fox – most of the time through binoculars – for something like a quarter of an hour. He was lying in the sun, having a nap, probably on the Thornthwaite Crag side of Threshwaite Cove, and we were coming down off John Bell's Banner. After we had watched him asleep for as long as we wished we decided to watch him on the move so we gave him a shout. He got up quite slowly, looked around at us and then started to amble leisurely up the slopes of Thornthwaite Crag, taking the steep slope in nicely graded zigzags. Every now and again he stopped and looked back at us, but he never hurried, and we watched him all the way, now and again carefully crossing a snow drift, until he passed over the summit and made off towards High Street.

On the same day we watched four or five red deer climb out of Rigindale and pass over High Street down to Hayeswater. Perhaps the wind was blowing towards us for they did not see us for a moment or two, and we were able to enjoy the sight of these lovely animals grouped most effectively on the summit ridge. Then somebody made a noise and they were off in a flash, bounding in great leaps down to the tarn and out of sight.

CENTRAL BUTTRESS
15 January 1954

Just forty years ago this spring the most remarkable achievement in British rock climbing up to that time was carried out on a tremendous, vertical crag in the heart of the Lake District, and a great sport, which is still a subject for controversy, entered a new era.

The crag was the impressive north face of Scafell, which faces the summit slopes of Scafell Pike, the climb – as any present-day climber will tell you – was Central Buttress (C.B., for short), and the climbers were Siegfried Herford (the leader), G.S. Sansom and C.F. Holland. The climb was the most daring ever achieved in this country, and although several harder routes have since been done in the Lake District and in North Wales, Central Buttress still remains a climb of great severity and character and will always be regarded as one of the really 'great' climbs in Britain.

In these days, when more people are climbing steep rocks than ever before, when the standard of British mountaineering has reached its highest standard so far and when ill-informed criticism is so often heard, it may be rewarding to look back on this great

Scafell Crag

achievement of 1914, for in many ways this was the start of rock climbing as it is practised today.

Some young rock climbers nowadays lay themselves open to criticism and on occasions have given a noble sport a bad name. Not a few are gymnasts, not mountaineers. They are not really interested in mountains but only in thrills, rather like 'wall of death' motor cyclists. Although not lacking in courage, a few are inclined to neglect elementary precautions. Sometimes they come to grief, and the general public is liable to condemn rock climbers altogether. A few of these young people are too prone to boast of their performances in public, and some of us have even heard them bragging of their falls instead of being ashamed of them.

But fortunately for the future of the sport in the Lake District and elsewhere, these people whose courage is being misapplied are not truly representative of the sport, and this small, reckless minority cannot claim to be the successors of Herford and his friends. Men like Herford and the great climbers of the past were mountaineers and lovers of mountain beauty, not merely rock gymnasts; they were excessively modest about their exploits; and they were painstakingly careful, knowing their own limitations with an exactness that comes only from experience.

Herford, a friend of Mallory who died on Everest, was undoubtedly a great man, besides being a magnificent climber, and it was one of the tragedies of British climbing that he should be killed in action in France in the First World War. Sansom and Holland, one a university professor, the other a schoolmaster, are both alive, I believe, and I have climbed with them both. To Holland, a man of great culture and imagination, Herford was the greatest man he had ever known.

Before the era climaxed by the ascent of Central Buttress, rock climbing in the Lake District – and, indeed, in Britain – was concentrated on the discovery of the easiest routes up vertical cliffs and the ascent of gullies, chimneys, ridges and other 'natural' ways up crags. The new era brought the forcing of routes up the great open walls between the gullies and later the traversing of the crags, and modern climbing is the development of this technique to the farthest limits of possibility.

Central Buttress goes up the centre of the crag for 470 feet in a series of steep walls and delicate traverses, and the crux of the climb is the ascent of the 65 feet high Flake Crack, which is mostly vertical and is slightly overhanging at the top. The whole route is sensationally exposed. When Herford and his companions finally climbed the Flake Crack, after several unsuccessful attempts, it was done by the leader standing on the shoulders of his second, as he (the second) hung in loops of rope just below the overhanging portion. This method (there are several variations) is still used by most people tackling the climb.

Once on the top of the Flake, the climber finds himself on a remarkable knife edge of rock, with a tremendous drop to the screes below and the difficult traverses above.

Herford's first reconnaissance of the buttress was made in January 1914, and the ascent was completed on 22 April on a snowy afternoon. The second ascent of Central Buttress was not made until August 1921, the leader being the late C.D. Frankland and his second, Bentley Beetham, the well-known mountaineer, who has pioneered scores of Lake District climbs and has climbed in the Himalayas.

In 1925 Dr Mabel M. Barker of Caldbeck accomplished the first ascent of the climb by a woman, and in August 1931 a most remarkable climber, Dr J.M. Edwards, made the first ascent of the route without assistance at the Flake Crack, a feat that has since been repeated a few times.

I believe that R.J. Birkett, the well-known Little Langdale climber, made the first ascent of Central Buttress in nailed boots – previous ascents had been made in rubber shoes – and the first woman to lead Central Buttress was Mrs S.H. Cross of the Dungeon Ghyll Hotel, Great Langdale. I think it was in 1936 that the first descent of Central Buttress was made, the last man on the rope being J. Carswell of Workington, and the first, appropriately enough, being Dr Barker, then fifty years of age.

New starts and new finishes have also been made to the original route, and nowadays Central Buttress is ascended several times each summer, but it is still a climb for experts in tip-top condition.

People who have seen Central Buttress at close quarters or, better still, have climbed it can realise something of the courage and tenacity of the young man who first led it in days when nothing of this severity had been attempted in Britain before. Holland has since written of Herford as 'the finest and bravest man I have ever known', and he knew him better than anybody else.

I would like to think of Herford's example of modest self-effacement, his quietness of manner and his balanced caution when climbing being followed by the climbers of today. So far as I know Herford never once fell from a climb.

CLIMBERS' FRUIT
7 May 1954

I cannot remember having eaten bilberries in early May before, but I did so last Sunday and enjoyed them, although they were not quite ripe. They were growing about 1,500 feet up in Longsleddale and growing in such profusion that you could have spent a whole day picking them without moving more than a few yards.

Perhaps some of my botanist readers will be able to tell me whether this abundance of early bilberries has anything to do with the possibility of a fine summer. Probably it is merely the result of our sunny April.

Bilberries are the climbers' fruit, for they normally grow on comparatively inaccessible ledges and are the just reward for great toil. There is Bilberry Chute, at the foot of Gimmer Crag in Langdale, and a Bleaberry Tarn, underneath the summit of Red Pike

Longsleddale

in Buttermere. Bleaberry and blaeberry are, I believe, alternative names for the same fruit. Sometimes the bilberry is known as the whortleberry, and there is also the red whortleberry, with fruit the size of a currant and a very tough skin, which bears no resemblance to the soft skin of the bilberry.

A plant similar to the red whortleberry is the bearberry, and this is also said to grow in Lakeland, although I do not know it myself. The crowberry, which has black berries, is common enough in Scotland, and there are also several other berries that grow among the mountains. A well-known berry in some of the Pennine districts is the cloudberry, which has bright red fruit. At one time it flourished well above the 2,000 foot contour among the rocks near the summit of Bowfell. The same plant is known in Scotland as the knowtberry and in some districts, I believe, as the roebuckberry.

Another of the red mountain berries is the cranberry, which is more often found in boggy ground. Sometimes red whortleberries or cowberries are sold as cranberries, and I have been told that bilberry is sometimes known as the lingberry or the crakeberry. Ling is really another name of heather, and generally heather and bilberries grow fairly close together. A good bilberry is covered with a bloom, just the same as a damson, and a handful of them, each one as big as a blackcurrant, can be a welcome mouthful on a hot day. I am informed that eaten in any quantity they bring on headaches and dizziness, but this I refuse to believe.

ENJOYING THE
LAKELAND FELLS
11 March 1955

The best way of enjoying the Lakeland fells, provided you know your own capabilities and limitations, is to travel them alone, and the best time to do so, given the requisite experience, is now, during the winter or in the early days of spring. There are now no crowds to disturb your contemplation; the colours, with the snow throwing the dullest shades into bright relief, are at their best; and it is cold enough to keep you moving without discomfort and bracing enough to induce the most wonderful feeling of wellbeing. Summertime, with its crowded hills, its dull colours, its restricted views due to haze, its enervating heat and its trails of orange peel and paper bags, has only one real advantage – its longer days.

From the valleys last Sunday looked a poor day – very cold with snow showers, racing clouds and a biting wind – but up aloft the day had its rewards for those willing to grasp them. It was too windy for skiing, too cold for rock climbing, and you need a companion for winter mountaineering in the gullies. I happened to be on my own that day, so I went for a walk over the tops, choosing the area I have known intimately since boyhood – the Coniston Fells. It is just thirty years ago since I first went up Coniston Old Man. I was on my own then, it was at the end of a 20 mile bicycle ride, with the same distance to ride home again, and it was my very first mountain. Since then I have probably been over those fells at least a hundred times and climbed on all their crags at all seasons of the year, yet on Sunday the familiar fells seemed just as new as ever.

There were a score of new things to see and enjoy: a long-forgotten view round a corner of rock, a rare patch of sunlight on a distant snow slope, cloud shadows racing the whole length of a valley, a frozen waterfall, snow formations caused by a freakish wind, the crusted ice on the familiar ledges of Dow Crag, an angry sunset across the Duddon valley and the flight of the geese over Harter Fell.

And there will always be something new to see on these fells – and on all the Lake District fells – if you are interested enough to look for them.

The whole tour, from Kendal and back again, took only a little over seven hours – about five and a half hours walking – and I did not hurry. No doubt I could have easily shortened this time by an hour, and many people could have cut it down by two hours, although they might not have seen quite so much. I went over seven or eight tops of round about the 2,500 feet mark, stopping when I felt like it, which shows what you can do when you are not wasting time by talking.

Church Beck is not the same as in the days of my youth, for the lovely wood was chopped down many years ago, but the derelict Copper Mines valley is still unchanged. I believe the project to flood this valley for hydroelectric purposes is still on paper in some official archives, and I still believe that an artificial lake in these parts would improve the scenery, besides being beneficial in more practical ways, but I am afraid I cannot say the same about other hydroelectric projects.

Many of the tremendous holes and caverns in the area have been fenced or boarded up, but there are still some places, notably near Simon's Nick, where a fall would mean quick death in depths from which a body would never be recovered.

Levers Water, reached by scrambling up the gill, proved to be well covered with good skating ice, in contradistinction to the surface on some of the more popular skating tarns this season, where the ice has been ruined by snow and wind. Near to Levers Water is a rock climb known as Sunlight Crack – not so called because the climb enjoys plenty of sunshine – and close at hand, on a piece of crag more often in shadow than otherwise, is the similarly named Sunshine Arete.

The three summits of Wetherlam were deserted, but after descending to Prison Band I met two young men coming down off Swirl How – the only people I met all day – who observed that it was a very cold day. Up to that time I had not felt the cold for I had kept on the lee side of the ridge going up Wetherlam, the northeast wind was at my back going up Swirl How, and I was well equipped with windproof clothing. Some time later, however, after ticking off the surrounding summits, I had to pass along the exposed shoulder of Brim Fell, and here the wind was biting. My eyebrows iced up completely, and my stockings went as hard as boards. It was difficult to see straight ahead, but it was exhilarating to press on to the summit of Coniston Old Man, where something approaching a blizzard was blowing.

I was reminded of a winter ascent some years before the war of this normally mild summit. On that occasion there was more snow about on the fells than I can ever remember, and the wind was blowing with tremendous force. Every single landmark was

The summit of Coniston Old Man

completely hidden beneath the snow, and the snow was falling so
thickly that the sky was obscured.

We were wearing, I remember, balaclava helmets and snow
goggles with motor cycle helmets on top – anoraks were uncommon
in those days – and we had to take a compass bearing to find the
summit and rope up for the last, normally inoffensive slope. The
huge summit cairn – in those days one of the biggest in the Lake
District – was completely buried, and we estimated there was
between 15 and 20 feet of snow on the top that day. It was nothing
like that last Sunday, but all the same it was cold enough.

I hurried down out of the wind to the col between the Old Man
and Dow Crag – noticing in passing that Seathwaite Tarn, the Barrow
Corporation reservoir more than 1,000 feet below, was completely

frozen over – and then made my way to the top of the crag. All the gullies were well filled with snow, but the steep crag stood out black against the surrounding whiteness. Through the mist and the snow showers I could see Goat's Water, solidly frozen far below. There is no finer corrie in the Lake District than this wild cirque, which on any summer Sunday echoes with the sound of happy climbers' voices, but there was no sound this Sunday, except that of the wind whistling through the crags. Even the ravens were quiet.

It is strange that Dow Crag retains its spelling, even though it adjoins Buck Pike and every climber pronounces it 'Doe', but I will not enter further into this controversy, which has been a subject for argument for fifty years.

There were no footprints in the snow over the pass, which on many a Sunday during the summer becomes a rough-riding route for motor cycles. Most people will remember, as I do, the first time that a motor car was driven over this rocky pass, but few people will have seen – as I have – a one-legged motor cyclist and his machine high up on the summit of the Old Man. I think he must have reached there by way of the back of Dow Crag.

It was dusk as I passed along Little Arrow Moor, past the place where young Stephen Darbishire photographed his 'flying saucer', past the Druids' Circle, where there may have been human sacrifices centuries ago, and down the steep track above the railway station into Coniston village. How pleasant not to have a 20 mile bicycle ride ahead of me.

BLACK COMBE
29 April 1955

To tens of thousands of people the most familiar mountain in the Lake District is not the symmetrically shaped Great Gable, massive-shouldered Scafell Pike or the huge hump of Helvellyn but the sprawling, whale-backed hump standing guard over the Duddon estuary and known as Black Combe. Perhaps some people would not call Black Combe a mountain – its summit stands 31 feet below the

2,000 foot contour line – but in bulk and grandeur, in its isolation and in the view from its cairn it is much more of a mountain than many higher peaks.

You can see Black Combe from the sitting rooms of houses in Morecambe, and I am told you can also see it from the tower of Liverpool Cathedral and from the mountains in North Wales. You can see it from Scotland, from the North Pier at Blackpool and from a score of places along the Lancashire coast as a great lump of fell standing on its own, a proud, dominating mass of moor and mountain.

Throughout my boyhood I lived almost in the shadow of Black Combe. Although the mountain was 6 miles away as the crow flies, it sometimes seemed no distance away at all and appeared to fill the whole view. We could see the little crags around the combe – we believed as youngsters that it was an extinct volcano – the lines of its ravines, the bracken and the heather and even the farms at its foot. This was a bad sign, for if Black Combe was so clear it would probably rain the next day.

Then there were times when we could not see the mountain for days or even weeks because of mist and rain, and other better days when the sun shone on its snows or the shadows of the clouds raced across its sunlit summit. Sometimes we looked at Black Combe across the water and thought we could row over in half an hour, and sometimes, from the highest point nearest my home, we traced the coastline around the Duddon estuary and across the foot of the mountain and watched the smoke of the trains as they chugged along past Green Road.

Black Combe was, of course, my first mountain – it was always a mountain to us. We did not know there were easier ways to the top. We just went straight up from some point along the Whicham valley road and carried on until there was nowhere higher to go. To a small boy it was a very big mountain. I thought we were at the top three or four times, and then we would see another lump of fell even higher. From the top we saw the peninsular spread out below us like a map. To the northeast lay the Lake District mountains, but the only tops I could recognise were the Coniston fells and, I seem to remember, the little triangle of Stickle Pike, which we had been up as first form schoolboys a few weeks earlier.

The other day, more than thirty year later, I returned to Black Combe, but this time, showing much less initiative and energy, I circumnavigated it by motor car. Unless you include fells like Wansfell Pike or Gowbarrow Fell, there are few, if any, Lake District mountains you can motor round in the same way as you can Black Combe. I am not suggesting, for one moment, that this is a good thing.

I went along the road over Bootle Fell, which is in better condition than when I last went that way many years ago, and completed the circle by way of the coast road and the road through the Whicham valley. Black Combe still looked a big chunk of fell – its area is much greater than that of many higher Lake District mountains – but it did not seem to have a great deal of character, although the slopes I had crawled up as a boy looked steep enough. Black Combe is certainly a mountain of character, but only when it is seen from afar or when enjoying the view from its summit.

The oldest rocks of which the Lake District is made are among the oldest rocks in the world, and the oldest rock of them all is called Skiddaw Slate. Black Combe is made out of Skiddaw Slate and is one of the oldest mountains in the world. The rock of which it is formed was laid down something like 500,000,000 years ago, which is a long time even to a geologist.

Was it Wordsworth who said that from the summit of this modest fell you can get the best and longest view in England? Whoever it was, he was probably correct. I have heard it said that you can see fourteen counties from the summit, and it is claimed that the view from the summit to Jack Hill, near Hanley in Staffordshire, is the longest continuous overland view in England. On a particularly clear day you may see from the summit the hills of Galloway in Scotland, the peaks of Snowdonia and eastern Wales, the Isle of Man and the mountains of Eire, but this is not exceptional, for I have seen all these from the summit of Scafell. You can see Black Combe from ships leaving the Mersey, and from the summit of the mountain on a clear day you can pick out shipping in many parts of the Irish Sea.

Swinside Stone Circle

The old Whitehaven road across the back of Black Combe, over which we drove the other day, is a real smugglers' road, and it is strange to reach the highest point above the 1,300 foot contour and look down on the chimneys of the atomic energy station down in the northwest.

This is also a countryside with a past, a distant past, which even today is full of mystery. Perhaps we will never learn the meaning of these ancient stone circles, old burial grounds and the remains of strange rites practised long before History began. Men came to these parts from the Continent in the Bronze Age and perhaps earlier, and today you can still see the signs they left behind them. Long before the Celts there was a village on these bleak slopes, and scattered around are burial cairns and even fortified positions. Most people have heard of the Swinside Circle, only half a mile away from a good road, but not many people take the trouble to go there. And there were once at least five other stone circles in the same neighbourhood. Few of the stones remain – they have been removed by farmers or blasted away to make stone for walls before they could be properly studied and recorded. Perhaps we have lost much knowledge of our earliest days through this ignorance or thoughtlessness.

But today, when you bump along this ancient road through a deserted countryside of a long-forgotten age, there is little to remind you of the past. You must seek it out.

Black Combe may be the oldest mountain in the world and these old stones may be full of meaning, but a Herdwick nuzzling in the bracken and a curlew hopping across the stony track in front of the car bring you back to the fun of being alive in Lakeland on a sunny day, not far below the clouds.

ONE MAN'S WAY
27 May 1955

Once every week for two years and on every day of every holiday a quiet, middle-aged Kendal man has been out and about on the eastern fells of the Lake District – almost always alone – exploring, writing, sketching and photographing and collecting the results in a bulky pocket book. Two or three days ago this long labour of love, together with hundreds of hours of patient, painstaking work in the quiet of his study at night, came to splendid fruition with the publication of what I sincerely believe to be the most remarkable book of its kind about the Lake District ever printed.

The book is remarkable first of all because every page – the text, the lovely drawings, the accurate maps, the revealing diagrams – have all been penned by the author and then printed from 300 engravings. It is further remarkable in that each of the 300 illustrations – drawings, diagrams and maps – are correct to the smallest detail. No book about the Lake District has ever carried this tremendous wealth of detail before. Perhaps no greater example of one man's patience in the sphere of a book production has been seen since the days of those beautifully illuminated books done by the monks of years ago.

Even if you have no interest whatever in the Lake District you will be staggered by this book, by the care and effort that have gone into its production and also by the remarkable fact that the book is only the first of a series of seven.

Let me tell you more about the modest author and this latest addition to Lakeland literature. He is forty-eight-year-old Mr Alfred Wainwright, for the last seven years borough treasurer of Kendal, and his book is the first volume, *The Eastern Fells*, of *A Pictorial Guide to the Lakeland Fells* (Henry Marshall, Low Bridge, Kentmere, Westmorland, 12s 6d).

Mr Wainwright, a Lancashire man, has been exploring the Lake District fells for twenty years, but something over two years ago he decided to examine them minutely and to record his impressions in notebook form. He had no thought of publication. He divided the whole area into seven parts and decided to make a start with the area most easily accessible by bus from Kendal. This is the area, covering about 50 square miles of territory, bounded on the west

Blencathra
from Clough Head

by the deep trough of Dunmail Raise and Thirlmere, to the east by the trench of Kirkstone Pass and Ullswater, and to the north by the broad Keswick to Penrith gap. This is the area covered by his first book. His second, on which he is now working, will be called *The Far Eastern Fells*, and, all being well, five others dealing with the whole of Lakeland will follow in their turn.

Mr Wainwright is not greatly concerned about valleys, lakes and villages. His great interest is the fells, and in his book he deals, in the very greatest detail, with thirty-five of them, from lordly Helvellyn and its satellites to little-visited Great Mell Fell, from mighty Fairfield and its fine precipices to Nab Scar, which the Lakes poets knew so well. It makes little difference – except in length of description – whether the fell is a fine mountain or a humble hillock; each one receives the same complete and careful treatment.

Each fell is illustrated by lovely line drawings – accurate, often dramatic and always artistic – by carefully drawn maps showing all possible routes, by diagrams indicating special points of interest, by smaller drawings of crags, cairns, waterfalls and so on, and by most detailed indications of the views from the summits. We are shown full panoramas in the form of outline drawings of the views from eight points of the compass or in other ways, such as concentric circles with the distant mountains accurately plotted. The text is detailed, informative, even amusing at times.

Mr Wainwright, as I have said, had no intention at first of publishing his notebook. He was persuaded to do so later by friends who realised that nothing so painstakingly complete, so beautifully finished, had ever been done before. Incidentally, although the author is the most unassuming of men, it is pleasant to discover in the Clough Head section a self-portrait – typically, a back view.

It would be niggardly of me to criticise a book that is going to give a great deal of pleasure to thousands of people, but I have already told the author that he runs the risk of taking all the adventure, all the joy of discovery, out of the fells by the very completeness of his work. His answer to this is that publication of his own discoveries – many of them never before mentioned in print – will encourage other fell-walkers to rediscover them for themselves.

He also poses many questions – 'Who cut this strange path across the fells and with what purpose?' – and deliberately leaves them unanswered. People purchasing the book will have to decide for themselves whether to use it as a guide, treasure it as an inspiring reference book or browse through it as a work of art.

Mr Wainwright made, on an average, six visits to each fell to collect his information and get the material for his illustrations and diagrams, but he went up Raise eight times before he had a view from the summit. On his trips he has taken many hundreds of photographs – not for publication but to help him with his illustrations, which in each case have been checked and elaborated on the spot.

His panoramas to show the hundreds of summit views have also been drawn from photographs and checked and double-checked both on the spot and at home, on the map, with compass and protractor. All the maps have been accurately reproduced by hand – in most cases to the scale of 2 inches to the mile – from the 2½ inch map, and the book is charmingly dedicated to 'the men of the Ordnance Survey'.

The hand-printing of the text is a work of art in itself – delightfully readable and attractive. Each page had to be done at least twice, and each line is carefully planned. You will notice, for instance, that each line finishes exactly on the margin with no parts of words carried onto the line below. Not one piece of type has been used, even for the embossing of the cover. All had been done by hand, for it was originally intended as a personal notebook only.

Mr Wainwright is now hard at work on his second book, and he tells me that the whole project, the seven books, will take him perhaps ten years. 'One man's way,' as he says in his introduction, 'of expressing his devotion to Lakeland's friendly hills.'

May I wish him many happy days in his further journeyings in the Lakeland he loves so well.

COLOUR PHOTOGRAPHY
4 November 1955

Colour photography is a fascinating – although rather expensive – pastime, and it is nowhere more rewarding than in the Lake District, especially at this time of the year.

Rarely has Lakeland appeared more colourful than on the last two Sunday mornings, and the opportunities for colour work seemed almost inexhaustible. On the way to more strenuous activities I was finding simple, fascinating subjects every five minutes, and only the realisation that every exposure was costing me something like two shillings (to produce the final lantern slide) prevented me from 'shooting' nearly everything in sight.

The great advantage of colour to an indifferent photographer like myself is that the simplest subjects, requiring expert treatment in monochrome, can make wonderfully effective colour pictures provided your equipment is good. The colour makes the picture, and errors in composition and even in technique are not so important. A long line of white ducks swimming past a jetty at Sharrow Bay with the low fells above Watermillock reflected in the still, blue waters of the lake made one picture, and another was taken near the pier at Pooley Bridge, with a rowan tree and the sun glinting on an old stone wall in the foreground and the long miles of water and the distant Helvellyn range for contrast in the background. Then a low, whitewashed cottage with a sheepdog asleep in the sun under the porch, a little waterfall tumbling over the brown rocks near Swarth Beck and, from high up the fellside, the gold of the bracken below white clouds in a blue sky.

This Sunday I was in Borrowdale by half past nine in the morning, but for the very best views I should have been there two hours earlier. These bright autumn days in Lakeland, particularly when they follow rainy days, should be seized and enjoyed to the full. After rain there is a freshness about the colours and a clarity in the atmosphere that you do not get in the middle of a long dry spell.

Borrowdale has never looked lovelier than it did on Sunday morning. The lake perfectly mirrored the Derwent fells, the sun glinted on the rooftops in Keswick nestling under the blue hulk of

Borrowdale, from Castle Crag

Skiddaw, and the woods along the miles of the valley were a blaze of colour. The smoke from the chimneys of the farms at Grange and Rosthwaite slowly rose up the fellsides, the golden leaves and the grey-white trunks of the birches were there plain to see in the waters of the Derwent, and the patches of damp still clinging to Gate Crag after the previous day's rain glittered in the morning sun like jewels.

My camera was again busy on the simpler features of the scene: the rich colouring of an old stone barn backed by a great oak tree, a shepherd with three dogs at heel working through the bracken, and looking through the reeds at Dale Head Tarn, the long valley of Newlands with the Causey Pike range for backcloth.

Colour photography has increased my appreciation of the simpler things in Lakeland: the yellows, browns and orange in an old stone wall, the greens, blues, purple and gold in the waters of a lonely tarn, the contrast of the bracken with the bilberry and the rich splendour of the autumn woods just before the leaves have disappeared.

NAPES NEEDLE
3 February 1956

Just about ten years ago there died far from the hills, in distant Dorset, a lonely old man whose name will be revered in Lakeland and in many places scattered about the world so long as men come to climb the rocks and walk the mountains.

His name was Walter Parry Haskett-Smith, and when he died, far from his friends, he was eighty-five years old. He was the 'father' of British rock climbing, the pioneer of the very earliest routes on half a dozen different Lakeland crags, and the man who first discovered and climbed Napes Needle.

Haskett-Smith first saw the Needle, a graceful pinnacle among the Napes Ridges on the Wasdale face of Great Gable, on a windy, cloudy day in the early 1880s. He has written: 'The outermost curtain of mist seemed to be drawn aside, and one of the fitful gleams of sunshine fell on a slender pinnacle of rock standing out against the background of cloud, without a sign of any other rock near it and appearing to shoot up for about 200 to 300 feet.'

At that time nobody had ever examined the Napes Ridges – the steep slopes of scree below them had kept explorers away and given the impression that the whole crag was dangerously rotten. But Haskett-Smith, the young Oxford graduate and barrister, decided to track down the slender spire and climb it if possible. At his first attempt he failed to locate it, but at the second he found it but left its conquest to another day.

Some years later he was exploring on the mountain quite alone and decided to work his way down from the summit to the ridge, now known as Needle Ridge, up which he had climbed two years before. He had with him a long fell pole, which gave him some trouble by continually dropping and jamming in cracks and crevices, but eventually he got down to the gap behind the Needle and decided, as climbers say, to 'have a look at it'.

There was nobody about on the mountain to help if he was to fall, and there were no mountain rescue teams in those distant days, but without hesitation the young man began to work his way up the tall spire, which seems to hang over Styhead. At first he used for his

Napes Needle, Great Gable

fingers and toes a crack, which in those days was blocked with stones and moss, and eventually he reached what is called the shoulder of the Needle and could study the final problem.

The summit of the Needle really consists of two tremendous blocks, one perched on top of the other, but the young man had no real means of knowing whether the top block was secure or whether, if pulled on, it would overbalance and crash with its victim to the screes 100 feet below. Today, of course, we all know it is safe, and if three climbers balance on one side it can be gently rocked, but on this day seventy years ago only two or three people had even seen the Needle and nobody had climbed it.

The young man was also anxious to know whether the summit of the top block was reasonably flat so that he could perch on it, in the event of his getting there. But, even more important, he thought that a flat top would mean that the edges of the top block would not be rounded and so would give him a good grip for his fingers. He therefore cast about for two or three flat stones and threw these up in turn, hoping that one would stay on top. At last one did so and he started up, 'feeling as small as a mouse climbing a millstone'.

He balanced himself up onto the Mantelshelf, with the steep drop on his right, shuffled along a horizontal crack, sidled round a corner, up the face on small holds and then, reaching up for the top, clambered up to the summit and sat down on his tiny, airy perch.

The summit of the Needle is a sloping oblong, only a few feet across, and when you are sitting or standing up there it is easy to imagine yourself very high above the world and almost sitting out in space. This sort of perch is common enough in the Alps but very rare in Lakeland, and there is nothing quite like the Needle anywhere else in the British Isles. People have stood on their heads on top of the Needle, lit fires up there, shaved and done a hundred and one other strange things, but Haskett-Smith just sat down, admired the view – and wondered how on earth he was going to get down.

Before he began lowering himself down, he left his handkerchief jammed in a crevice for all to see, and it must have been something of a relief and a moment of pride to get down the top block safely and be able to look up at the bit of linen fluttering in the breeze.

Since those days the Needle has been climbed thousands of times by seven or eight different routes, it is photographed dozens of times every week during the summer, and its shape is known in many parts of the world. Small boys and girls have been hauled up it in fine weather, stunt climbs and silly record attempts have been made on it, it has been filmed and televised, painted and sketched, but the Needle – although nowadays regarded as a comparatively easy route – is still a climb of character and a remarkable memorial to a very great man.

On the fiftieth anniversary of his first ascent of the Napes Needle, Haskett-Smith, then a man of seventy-four, went up again, roped between Lord Chorley and the late Mr G.R. Speaker. Many hundreds of people, sitting and standing on the rocks around, watched the slow, careful ascent on Easter Sunday 1936, and when the old man clambered onto the top of the most famous bit of rock in English climbing the crowd below him gave a cheer.

Haskett-Smith had a reputation of never being at a loss for words, and his gift for repartee did not fail him even on this particularly important occasion. 'Tell us a story,' shouted someone from the crowds below, and the old man seated on the spire a hundred feet above their heads replied, in a flash: 'There is no other story. This is the top storey.'

This fine mountaineer had climbed in the Alps, Norway, the Pyrenees, North Africa, the Balkans, the Rockies and the Andes, but it was on Lake District climbing that he left his most permanent mark. He was a man of strong personality, a brilliant speaker and a man of wide reading and culture, but often eccentric in his habits and dress. At formal evening functions he would often appear, without the slightest embarrassment, in the most careless array, while for open-air excursions he would turn out, on the hottest days, in a long, heavy, check tailcoat fitted with huge outside pockets.

Nobody can be claimed as the 'inventor' of British rock climbing, but this tattered Old Etonian, with his ragged moustache and a glint in his eye, probably came nearer than anybody else. Men of his individuality are not so often seen today, and I often regret that I never met him. He was little seen in the Lake District after the First World War, and some of the modern generation of young rock climbers have perhaps never even heard of him. But his name will be kept green by a little-climbed gully named after him, a couple of slim books on climbing, a few articles and Napes Needle, in a way the finest memorial that anyone could have.

NEW BEAUTY
16 November 1956

How many of you, I wonder, noticed the view across Windermere from near Low Wood on Sunday morning? I suppose this is perhaps the most hackneyed view in the whole of Lakeland – the first uninterrupted sight of the upper lake, backed by the Coniston fells and the Langdale Pikes, to be seen by the visitor from Lancashire or Yorkshire – but on Sunday this was no ordinary picture. There was no wind whatever at lake level, and the water was exactly like a huge looking-glass. Across the far side of the lake a long band of thick, white mist hung almost motionless across the fells, leaving the summits shining in the morning sunshine and, below the band, the meadows, the woods and the clustered farms with the smoke rising straight from the chimneys.

The distant rock turrets above Langdale glinted and sparkled as if on fire, and the long summit of Wetherlam, below a blue sky chased with orange clouds, looked hardly a fraction of its 6 miles away. The whole picture, with the golden-yellow of the autumn leaves, the browns and the blues of the sky and the rocks, with the great white scarf hanging across the hills, was exactly mirrored in the lake. And everything so quiet and peaceful that even a bird alighting on the water might have spoiled the effect.

We stopped for ten minutes or so to try and capture the perfection on colour film, and during those few minutes every car passing in either direction stopped so that the occupants could admire the view.

I suppose I must have seen this view thousands of times – probably at least half a dozen times every week – but it is rare that I pass that way without noticing some new beauty. It is never quite the

Windermere, at Low Wood

same. Each week of the year brings new colouring, new lighting, new shadows, and yet this is supposed to be a commonplace view, only one out of hundreds. One need never grow tired of Lakeland. There will always be new beauty if one cares to look for it.

I don't think the Lake District has ever looked more lovely than during the last month of perfect autumn weather. How unfortunate are those people who see Lakeland only during the crowded, often wet and colourless holiday months of July and August.

FOR THE UNFORTUNATE ONES
22 February 1957

To most of my readers the fell country is a place of happy memories, a homely corner to which they return again and again, a countryside that even a faded photograph or, perhaps, an old rucksack readily recalls. These are the people for whom I am particularly writing today – the unfortunate ones who do not see the Lakeland hills every day.

As I write, the hills are looking their very best, and perhaps a few of you living among the smoke and grime of towns might be interested in one or two February peeps into the sanctuary. From my window I can see the Kentmere fells, rising white and shining beyond a nearby larch wood. The shoulder of Lingmell End merges into the broad back of High Street, and the beetling face of Rainsborrow Crag, where the foxes play, shows dark against the sunlit fells.

The snow lies thick down to the 1,000 foot contour and glistens in the sunshine. In some places the snow melts in the sun for a few hours each day but starts to freeze up again about three o'clock in the afternoon. But there are places facing northeast never reached by the sun, and here the snow is lying, fluffy and powdery, just as it fell.

No doubt the snow that falls in Lakeland is the same sort of stuff that comes down in Preston or Blackburn, but the similarity ends there. As we all know, snow in the towns rapidly becomes dirty slush, but on the high fells it is altogether a very different thing – at its best, a lovely dry powder, which does not seem wet or cold and which you can shake off your clothes as easily as dandruff.

The head of Kentmere

Blanketed with snow the Lakeland hills – and indeed any hills – look bigger and much more impressive. Three days ago I was driving along the main Windermere to Kendal road. From one point along this road there is a good view of the Sedbergh fells – the Howgills, as we call them – but few people ever stop to admire the view for the hills are not particularly interesting. But on this day they were covered in snow, and, like many others, I stopped the car to enjoy the picture.

The hills looked twice their height, you could see every wall and every outcrop of rock – there are very few of either – and the slopes appeared chiselled out of ice. Some of the blue from the sky was reflected in the shadows on the snow, and the moulding and the sculpture were most impressive. I could trace a ski tour I once made along these fells, and I remembered falling through a snow bridge over a hidden stream on the way down. Very undignified it was, upside down in two to three feet of water with my skis wrapped round my neck.

Blencathra is one of the finest looking mountains in the Lake District when the snow lies on the fells. Last Sunday it looked like an Alpine giant, with its long ridges thrown into sharp relief by the snow and its normally inconspicuous crags appearing quite impressive. One of the photographs of Mr W.A. Poucher showing the ridges of Blencathra deep in snow is a particularly striking example of the effect of snow on the Lakeland fells.

Most visitors to the Lake District – including many who consider themselves to be knowledgeable about the area – never see the fells under the snow. They can have no idea of their winter beauty: the extraordinary distances one can sometimes see in February, the contrasts between the white and the blue of the snows and the browns, the oranges and the soft colourings in the valleys, and the truly remarkable sunsets. A few of us saw one such sunset last Sunday. We were skiing down through mist from the summit of Raise towards Thirlspot and, after crossing Fisher Gill, climbed up out of the dip, out of the mist and into strong evening sunshine. The crisp snow at our feet sparkled in the sunset, the Thirlmere valley below glowed darkly, the snow on the western hills was flecked with gold and a great fiery sky promised another fine day to come.

An hour before, from the summit, we had been identifying dozens of the Lakeland hills, all of them looking much different under snow but easy enough to pick out. Even a comparative stranger to the Lake District would probably have been able to identify Great Gable, with its characteristic sugar loaf shape, rearing up above the Borrowdale fells, rather like some remote peak in Alaska.

It is on these days when there are so few people about on the fells that one has a chance of seeing more of the wildlife. For instance, the other day I saw a fine red stag in Longsleddale, the nearest I have seen one yet to Kendal although I know they come down this valley on occasions. Five minutes before I had just taken the last exposure of a colour film. It was of a fine waterfall in the Sprint below Goat Scar, with the spray dancing over the rocks and the sun shining into the pool. I was annoyed that I could not photograph the stag for, as the wind was blowing straight at me, I thought I would be able to get close to him. This I was able to do, until I disturbed a stone. He looked round at me, stared at me for a second and then decided to leave. Without any effort he sailed over a 5 foot dry stone wall and then trotted slowly down into Mosedale.

I watched him for five minutes at least. Twice he turned round, then carried on determinedly towards Swindale. A minute or two later my terrier, which had not seen him, picked up his scent and got very excited. I kept him back, for the stag was not going my way, but the little chap had his reward later on Harter Fell when he put up two rabbits.

It is always thrilling to see a red deer on the Lakeland fells, but in Scotland I have seen probably 200 or more in a day and thought nothing about it. Places where you can be sure of seeing red deer in Scotland in large numbers are the islands of Arran and Rum.

Perhaps it is even more exciting to see a fox at close quarters. I have had one jump out from underneath my feet – near the summit of The Screes above Wastwater – and I have twice watched a sleeping fox, but this weekend one passed within 3 yards of me and I did not see it. It was on the summit of Raise, and I was walking quite near to the ski tow machine. A friend made a sudden signal from about 50 feet away, but before I had realised what it was all about it was too late. Apparently a fox had darted across the snow just behind me, but he was gone in a flash and we never saw him again.

THE HIGH PLACES
27 February 1959

For more than a fortnight I have seen nothing of Lakeland, nor heard, nor read anything about it either, which, for me, is rather remarkable. Perhaps this is not strictly true. By raising myself on my pillow and screwing my neck round until it hurts I have just been able to see a corner of Rainsborrow Crag and the shoulder of Lingmell End at the head of Kentmere. There were two tiny snow patches up there the other afternoon.

And the other day, with kind wishes for my recovery, I had a little word picture of the Lakeland countryside from an old friend in Grasmere. 'Nice spring-like day this week,' he wrote. 'The birds are singing. I hear the curlews are going over today. The wild geese are uneasy. I see the wild swans are still with us. Fresh green leaves on the honeysuckle and the elder. The snowdrops are in flower.'

But this is all the information I have at present about the Lakeland that has been my life for as long as I can remember. As I write, it is damp, miserable and so foggy that I cannot see further than two fields away from the house. Yet when I was last in the hills, sixteen days ago – it seems like months – we sat, stripped to the waist, in the hot sunshine, nearly 3,000 feet up looking across the fells at Scotland beyond the Solway. And by a turn of the head we could see the broad, flat-topped Yorkshire hills.

With no new scenes or experiences to record, I thought I might draw on some of my earliest memories of Lakeland. My very first mountain, if you could call it that, was Black Combe, but my first summit was Stickle Pike, that miniature Matterhorn overlooking the Duddon valley, which is so prominent a feature of the long line of hills culminating in Coniston Old Man. I was a member of a school party and about eight years old, so it was about forty years ago.

We walked to Broughton Mills from Broughton (or Woodland, I cannot clearly remember), and when we got to the foot of our little mountain the master in charge made us eat our sandwiches before tackling the climb, which, I suppose, was sensible enough. I have a photograph of about twenty of us on the summit – bare knees and schoolboy caps with little knapsacks on our backs. The only other thing I remember about my first summit is that we all ran down helter-skelter from the top, except the master who picked his way slowly and was very annoyed about our lack of discipline. I'm afraid we did not bother with the view, and we thought it a very simple expedition, but we were tired enough before we got back to the train.

I have written before about Black Combe, which came about a year or two later, so will not deal with it again except to say that I still remember, after nearly forty years, the view from the summit across to the Lakeland hills and, in the other direction, the Furness peninsula spread out like a map. This was the view that Wordsworth thought the best of its kind in Lakeland.

Black Combe must have impressed me because after that we were always in the hills, exploring such places as quarry holes, ravines and woods, but it was the adventure and the excitement that were the attraction then, not so much mountain scenery. We had hideouts at the tops of trees, secret caves behind waterfalls and trysting places in many a dark, waterlogged quarry hole. All good boyish fun, but I have often regretted that we did not learn more at this time about the birds and the flowers and the trees, for a knowledge of these things is the basis of a love of the great outdoors. As it was, this information had to be acquired later, rather painstakingly and, in many cases, from books.

I think the first mountain I climbed especially for the view was Coniston Old Man, when I was about thirteen or fourteen years of age. I went up on my own after a bicycle ride of more than 20 miles to the foot of the mountain because I wanted to see what lay behind the Coniston fells. When I reached Torver I abandoned my original plan of cycling to Coniston and decided to go straight up from there as this seemed the more direct route. I finally gained the summit by

Dow Crag, Coniston

way of Cove quarries above the former gunpowder hut, which is not, by any means, a usual route, but I had nobody to tell me better and, I regret to say, no map.

The view from the summit amply repaid the long bicycle ride and the tiring struggle up the sliding quarry heaps. Almost the whole of Lakeland was spread out for me to see, and I spent a long time on top feasting my eyes on it and trying to identify the mountains. But the feature of the view that impressed me most of all was that of Dow Crag, due west across the corrie containing Goat's Water. I did not know it was Dow Crag then, and I only saw the great precipice after I had left the summit and was making my way down towards the Cove quarries by the way I had come. I remember there was a great black cloud hanging over the crag, then a patch of open sky, and then the tremendous precipice itself, dropping apparently vertically into a black tarn.

I had never seen anything like this before: it was awe inspiring, almost frightening. And as I came further down the fellside I heard voices coming down from the direction of the great black crag and saw tiny figures hurrying down the steep paths among the screes just above the tarn. All the way home I was thinking about what I had seen, and I soon found out the name of the crag and then began to devour every book on rock climbing and mountaineering I could find in the public library.

A year or two later I was taken on my very first rock climb and, appropriately enough, it was on this same crag – the popular Woodhouse's Route on B Buttress. There have been a number of 'firsts' since then – the first time I led a rock climb, my first Scottish peak, my first peak in the Alps, the first time I led a first ascent and so on – but the most significant of them all was, I believe, that humble ascent of Coniston Old Man, just to see the view. For that day I discovered mountain beauty and inspiration for the first time.

To the true mountain lover the hills are his whole life. For him the mountains, whether they are our little Lakeland hills or the giants of the Alps or the Himalayas, are a constant challenge, but – more important – they are always an inspiration to him to turn from false values to things that really matter. And the attraction of the hills is their beauty, for surely there is more beauty, more grandeur, more nobility in the higher places of this earth than there is among the flat lands.

To enjoy the hills to the full, the true mountain lover must know them and know everything about them. He must know them at all seasons of the year, and he must walk their ridges, climb their crags and ski across their snowfields. He must know about hill weather, the meaning of the wind and the clouds, and he must know the birds, the animals, the trees, the flowers and everything that grows and lives upon the hills. He must know about the hill people, their customs, traditions and sports, and he must know about the story of the rocks and how and why the hills came to be there. All these things and many more the true mountain lover must know, and he may spend his life learning them and still not know them all.

But once a man discovers the hills he has got hold of something that will stay with him to the end of his days. He will never tire of it and nobody can take it away from him, but he will be really happy only when he can lift up his eyes to the hills. Perhaps that is why I have been so miserable recently: so near to the hills and yet so far away. This flu germ has much to answer for.

GREAT GABLE
5 June 1959

Great Gable, some people say, is the finest mountain in England, both to look at and to look from. This claim and the fact that I have been scrambling about on Gable several times during the past few weeks suggest that a pen portrait of the mountain may not be out of place in these notes.

I suppose the view of the mountain that immediately springs to most people's minds is that from the shore of Wastwater as one approaches Wasdale Head, with Gable appearing as a shapely triangle between Kirk Fell (or Yewbarrow) on the left and Lingmell leading up to Scafell Pike on the right. Perhaps, indeed, this is the most photographed view in the whole of Lakeland, and it is the view that the Lake District Planning Board uses as the emblem for the National Park.

In this view, Gable appears graceful, serene and queenly, the natural centrepiece of the finest ring of fells in this country, and the dark waters of the lake with its rocky shoreline seem to set off a picture of calm majesty. Very often we see the shadows of the clouds chasing across the bare mountainside, and sometimes there is a wisp of cloud caught on the pointed summit. As we draw nearer to the most impressive valley head in England, we can see the thin scratch of the track over the Sty zigzagging up the fellside, and, if the day is clear enough and we know where to look, we can pick out the Needle, set among the clustered Napes ridges.

This is the popular view of Great Gable, but it is not necessarily the most typical. Many people will think of the mountain not as a graceful cone but as a rather ugly shaped hump, for this is its appearance from many other directions – from the Helvellyn range, for instance. And this is the view of Gable – a great, rounded lump thrusting into the sky, with the precipitous crags of the Napes and Gable Crag on opposite sides – that suggests its true character.

For Great Gable, no matter how friendly it may look from the patchwork fields in Wasdale head, is not really an elegant and smiling fell, but rather a bold, bare mountain, most unusually ringed with crags and screes on almost all its sides, independent, savagely moody at times and always challenging. It is a mountain of character, and the 'pretty pretty' pictures do it a disfavour.

Because all its sides are steep there is a feeling of airiness about Great Gable that one does not get from many other Lakeland mountains, even the higher ones. The best point from which to look

Great Gable, from Great End

out from Gable, they say, is from the cairn on Westmorland Crag, just below the summit on the 'popular' side, but this is a matter of choice. Last Sunday I was sitting on the Needle admiring the view and it was, as always, striking enough. There are sheer drops below on all sides and, with a little imagination, one can almost imagine oneself suspended in space. There is a feeling that one could almost throw a stone down to Wasdale head or, at any rate, to the foot of the mountain, while the fells around Wastwater, including the dark rampart of The Screes, look curiously flattened. The hotel, the farms and the tiny church amid the yew trees look like wooden models stuck onto a cardboard base of painted fields, and away in the distance, beyond the lake and the coastal plains, there is the sea, glittering, on Sunday at least, in the sunlight.

Only one other thing retains its stature and its majesty from this viewpoint and that is the great, black precipice of Scafell Crag hanging over the shoulder of Lingmell. Everything else bows down before the grandeur of the tumbled, soaring ridges where we sit.

Everybody who is interested knows the story of how Napes Needle was first climbed by W.P. Haskett-Smith in 1886 and how the great Owen Glynne Jones was stirred to begin his Lakeland climbing by the sight of a photograph of the Needle in a shop in The Strand.

I remember Haskett-Smith and I recall the occasion in 1936 when, as a man of seventy-four, he made his anniversary ascent. He was a man of extremely ready wit and quite composed in any situation. When he sat down on the topmost block to which he had first ascended, quite alone and the first man ever to do so, fifty years earlier, a voice came up from the crowd assembled on the ledges below, 'Tell us a story.'

The old man perched on his pinnacle shouted down without hesitation, 'There is no other story,' he told them. 'This is the top storey.'

Many very much harder climbs than the Needle have, of course, been made on Gable, but it is not only a climber's playground. Its summit, for ordinary walkers, is possibly the most popular in Lakeland, although the multiplicity of cairns in the area is quite unnecessary. A bronze plaque mounted among the highest rocks indicates the war memorial of a well-known climbing club, the actual memorial being the surrounding central summits of Lakeland, and a simple service is held there, no matter what the weather, every November.

There is often a pool of rainwater caught in these summit rocks even in time of drought, a little point worth remembering, for Gable can be a very dry mountain. There is, too, a tiny spring not far from Kern Knotts that I have never known to fail in well over thirty years. It was there on Sunday, after three weeks of dry weather, and my dog, which had been there a week or two earlier, trotted ahead of me to the spot and drank his fill in the tiny cave.

Gable Crag on the less-visited side of the mountain is a fine, north-facing precipice, which can be a delightful haven of solitude when the more popular climbs are too crowded for enjoyment. Some distance up this crag are the remains of what might have been a stone hut, and tradition has it that 'Moses', the illicit whisky distiller, used this as a hideout. Another theory is that it might have been used as a store for stolen wadd or plumbago from the mine near Seathwaite. Moses' Trod is the well-graded track that passes along the 'back' of Gable towards the top of Honister, and Moses' Finger is the prominent boulder at the top of the grass slope of Gavel Neese.

The stony track over the Sty, which winds across the face of Gable, is a romantic route, the only direct connection between the valleys of Borrowdale and Wasdale and a route that has probably little altered in the last few hundred years. On many occasions in the past a road has been threatened across this lonely pass, but such an 'improvement' can never come to pass, for the opposition is much too strong. The two valleys would be ruined if this sort of thing was ever tackled, and the tranquillity of the central fells would be lost forever.

Great Gable is the favourite Lakeland mountain of many people. To me it will also be a holiday mountain, for I spent many happy days there as a youth, climbing its airy ridges, racing down its screes, walking over the top by moonlight, bathing in nearby Styhead Tarn, searching for garnets in the boulders on the Wasdale side or striding down through the bracken after a hot, dusty day for tea and scones.

But for some it is a tragic mountain. Last weekend I was once again in the tiny church among the views and again I wandered in the churchyard and saw the climbers' graves. Two or three, but not all, were killed on Gable, but all knew the mountain well, and they lie there because they loved the hills. So, to me, Gable, although a holiday mountain, is not also the friendly, smiling mountain you see from the lake shore. It is a challenge and an inspiration, but it can also be a warning.

A WONDERFUL SUMMER
TO REMEMBER
23 October 1959

On a wet October afternoon, with the clouds almost down to the fields and the leaves swirling about in the puddles, it is pleasant to bring back memories of this most glorious Lakeland summer, the finest most of us can remember and one that may not be repeated for many, many years.

The dying bracken was a glowing russet carpet and the fells were brown and grey when I was in the hills the other day, but my principal memory of this summer's wonderful views is how blue everything has been – the lakes, the hills, the skies and the shadows. There is a particular colour process that tends to give some photographic transparencies an unnatural blue tinge, particularly those taken at a considerable altitude or across water, and as all photographers know, one can use filters to make the colours seem more correct. But this summer, it has seemed to me, we have been able to see, with the naked eye, an overall blueness that, if reproduced on a slide would be condemned as 'unnatural'.

Scientists, no doubt, can explain this phenomenon – perhaps it has something to do with the blueness of the skies or some particular quality of the atmosphere – and probably there is also some simple explanation for the unusually large amount of heather, blue heather, that we have had on the Lakeland hills this summer. In fact, what with the distant patches of hillside heather – there have been masses of it on Skiddaw, for instance – and the blueness of the lakes, becks, rocks and shadows, it has been easy, on several occasions this summer to imagine oneself in the northwest of Scotland, where the colours can be the most remarkable seen in Britain.

To those who think this Scottish reference a trifle exaggerated I would say that I once met, near Kylesku Ferry in Sutherland, a famous professional photographer who told me that in a lifetime's search for natural beauty he had never seen colours to approach those in that part of Scotland. I left him on his knees going nearly delirious about the incredible beauty of some water lilies in a blue lochan among the purple heather.

I remember being strongly reminded of Scotland one day this summer when coming down into Wasdale off Illgill Head after we

The Buttermere valley

had climbed one of the gullies in The Screes. The long, dark lake immediately below us, the unfenced road winding along the farther shore, the rocky slopes of Yewbarrow, Middle Fell and Buckbarrow sleeping in the heat haze, the summit of Gable just capped with cloud, and the solitude and stillness of everything, with not a soul or a motor car or a building in sight, were very reminiscent of Wester Ross, Knoydart or even Appin. We saw no other people that day, either on our climb or on the descent, although this was Wasdale, Lakeland's incomparable jewel, on a perfect Sunday in September.

Indeed, despite the crowded roads and the sunshine crowds, we have generally managed to find places where the solitude has been little disturbed. So, if that is what you want, you can still find it in Lakeland – provided you know where to look.

One afternoon we sat smoking in a sunny, bilberry-carpeted corner high up on the face of a great, grey crag not far from Coniston. It was one of the later days of summer, but the sun was beating down on the craggy fellside across the corrie and really glowing on the steep sweep of precipice below our feet. Tiny figures, like sawn-off matches, appeared briefly at the distant cairn and then disappeared – insignificant specks in a tumbled, soaring landscape. A bubble of laughter, caught by a rising zephyr, came winging up from coloured dots by the tarn nearly a thousand feet below us, and a sudden white flash on the blue, sunlit surface told of a late summer bathe.

Soundlessly, a raven shot out of the crag like a hurtled stone and rolled and looped over the combe, while thousands of feet up in the blue zenith a four-engined plane, like a tiny silver dart, moved slowly across the sky. A smoky haze lay over the distant, sleepy landscape, little winged insects whirred in the dry grass, and the only sound was the slither of moving scree, disturbed by some adventurous sheep, out of sight and far below.

I remember another stiflingly hot day in Langdale with the becks dried up and silent and the heat reverberating off the rocks like sound from a gong. All the way up Gimmer Crag we wondered if there could possibly be any moisture left in the little waterfall that splashes down through the moss a short distance below the precipice. There was no sound from the little streamlet, but just enough drips oozing out from the moss to maintain a pool the size of two cupped hands. We drained it dry – the two of us and the dog – and when we returned, perhaps four or five hours later, it had filled again, the only water on the great, bare fellside.

Between climbs on the great sweep of crag we lay down on grassy couches eating bilberries and listening to the distant whine of sports cars ascending the bends on the Blea Tarn road. This was another one of the 'blue days', with Bowfell and the Crinkles and the Coniston fells shimmering in the blue haze, but far below in Mickleden we could see where the river had been dammed and widened and we thought what a splendid swimming pool it would make if we were 2,000 feet lower down.

And there have been other splendid days on Scafell, Gable and Pillar with the rocks almost too warm to touch and the lichen so dry that one could stand confidently in rubber soles on the most minute holds. I cannot remember such a wonderful summer for rock climbing, and some of the very hardest routes have been done several times.

But last Sunday, we thought, was the last day of summer. It was a different day from most of the rest, and it was not long before we traced the reasons for this: the crowds had gone and the becks had returned to life. Although we have generally managed to find solitude on the fells, the valleys have been crowded all summer – until last Sunday.

The change was quite remarkable. No tents or caravans on the summit of Dunmail, none in Borrowdale and none in Buttermere. As my friend said to me as we drove along the almost deserted roads; 'Lakeland belongs to the visitors in summer; now it belongs to us.' We hardly saw a soul in Borrowdale, the usual rock climbs were deserted, and apart from one string of walkers on Honister, there was nobody all the way to Buttermere and the little car park was empty.

The previous night's rain had also brought about a wonderful change. There were becks foaming and gurgling everywhere down the fellside, and the Gatesgarthdale Beck came splashing and leaping underneath Honister Crag like a glacier torrent and about the same colour. All the way up to our climbs the fellsides were soaking, but a fresh breeze sent the clouds scampering high above the fells, kept off the rain and dried the crags.

We climbed on dry rock and looked across the lake and the Buttermere fells at Skiddaw, cloud capped and brooding. Four hours later we made our way back to the valley by walking along the ridge in half a gale. Pillar Rock, across the Liza and the massed conifers, looked dark and forbidding but too distant to be impressive, and the clouds hung low over the Scafells. Gable showed its uglier side, Kirk Fell looked massive and bumpy, Blencathra to the northeast just peeped over a shoulder of Robinson, Grasmoor looked a much more impressive mountain than it really is, and the long line of the Dodds and the Helvellyn range was just below the clouds.

It was good to be out on a high ridge in a high wind with the clouds racing across the sky, but we knew that the rain could not hold off much longer, so we wasted no time in trotting down to the valley and had no sooner reached the car than the downpour began. It was a wet drive home, and I remember, somewhere near Newlands Hause, the headlights picking out a lone Herdwick lying out in the driving rain by the side of the road. So this, we thought, was the last day of summer. The winter is now before us.

1960s

Pillar Rock

MAGNIFICENCE OF PILLAR ROCK
8 January 1960

The only great precipice in Lakeland that cannot be reached by the ordinary walker is Pillar Rock, the tallest lump of more or less vertical crag in England. It is a much bigger affair than Blackpool Tower and a thousand times more beautiful and inspiring, but it is the least visited of the major crags of the Lake District and probably completely unknown to the majority of casual visitors. Thousands of people who claim some familiarity with Lakeland have never even seen it.

Just before the old year went out three young students were marooned all night on the north face of this cliff, and dozens of volunteers were involved in their rescue in miserable weather the following day when they might have been more pleasantly employed preparing their New Year celebrations. Apart from making the rather obvious suggestion that the young people seem to have bitten off more than they could chew, I will not, in the absence of all the facts, attempt to judge their performance, but the occasion seems an opportunity for writing something about this remarkable example of Nature's architecture.

There seems to me to be several reasons why Pillar Rock is comparatively little known or visited. It lies at the head of Ennerdale, which has no public road and is one of the most desolate dales in the Lake District; it is separated by two hours' walking from the nearest base, and it is a relatively disappointing sight when seen from the surrounding fells. Hundreds of people, for instance, must have looked across the head of Ennerdale from the Buttermere fells and not even noticed the Rock, which has a habit of blending into its background, and from the summits of most of the mountains of Lakeland Pillar Rock is either unseen or unremarkable.

Even from the summit of Pillar, the mountain upon whose northern slopes the Rock is perched, the crag appears relatively insignificant, for one is looking down at its short southern side, and the tremendous drop down to the River Liza is not seen. Indeed, it is only when one approaches the crag from the Forestry Commission plantations or, better still, along the High Level Route from Wasdale that the great rock is seen in all its splendour.

The toil up the fellside from the jungle of conifers is steep, and even here, immediately below the crag, the Rock is out of sight for part of the way, but halfway up the great cone comes into view, and although greatly foreshortened, the sight of so much vertical rock makes one feel very small indeed.

The perfect approach is along the High Level Route, which contours along the side of Pillar Mountain, skirts little green coves, rises and falls across rocky ridges, and then reaches Robinson's Cairn, the memorial to a great mountaineer and Lakeland lover. And here one gets the best view of Pillar Rock. It rises straight ahead, a great cathedral-like structure but bigger than any cathedral in the world. A green ledge runs along its foot, and above it the great walls rise almost vertically for about 500 feet in height to Low Man, above which there is an upper section a few hundred feet in height leading to High Man, the small summit. The crag is flanked by other crags, with scree slopes in between, and there are only a few places in Britain – all of them in Scotland – where you can see more rock in one glance.

Viewed from this point, it is easy to understand why the Rock has always been an object of awe to the surrounding dalesfolk and why the very earliest guides to Lakeland referred to it as one of the district's most remarkable features. Wordsworth made it the scene of a fatal accident in his poem 'The Brothers', published 160 years ago, and for something like a hundred years the shepherds and farmers of western Lakeland must have discussed the rock's apparent impregnability.

Many people tried to reach the top, but it was not until 1826 – fifty years before the start of the sport of rock climbing – that an Ennerdale man, John Atkinson, succeeded in getting there. Although Atkinson probably reached the summit by what is nowadays known as the Old West Route, which is little more than a scramble, this was a most remarkable feat for he had to contend not merely with the difficulties of the route but also with all the accumulated fears and prejudices of his age.

The Old West Route goes up an easy rake, which runs up the centre of the steep western face to arrive at a point on Low Man. The dalesman, unaware of the importance of his exploration, would then have continued up the easy ledges and chimneys to High Man, but whether he felt any pride or awe to be the first man to reach there we do not know. But as he looked down the whole length of Ennerdale towards his home – there were no foreign conifers in the dale in those days – he must have felt a great exhilaration, for there is a great difference between the view from the usual Lakeland summit and that from the top of the Rock. In the one case you are sitting a-straddle the rooftops; on the other, you are perched on the weather vane of a church spire.

The year after Atkinson's feat three other local dalesmen reached the summit, and it is reasonable to assume that these men, all shepherds, knew the neighbourhood of the rock quite well and had scrambled about the sides rescuing their sheep. Down the years hundreds of sheep must have wandered down from Pillar Mountain to the Rock and then fallen to their deaths down such places as Walker's Gully and Shamrock Gully, and from time to time short stretches of wall have been built above the gullies to try and prevent these accidents.

It is estimated that up to a hundred years ago there had been about twenty-five ascents, and by 1875 more than a hundred, the first woman having reached the top in 1870. The total of ascents must now run into thousands. I first went up thirty years ago and must have made a score of ascents since, but some people I know have been up fifty or even a hundred times.

There are more than fifty routes on Pillar Rock today, ranging from easy scrambles, like Slab and Notch, to the extremely severe and exposed routes on the west face of High Man. You can reach the summit after 500 feet of steep, difficult climbing, or perhaps 200 feet of moderate scrambling, or even by routes of only 50 feet in length. This is what is wrong with Pillar Rock: its southern side, although vertical, is too short. From the summit one can drop down into Jordan Gap on a doubled rope in a few seconds or climb down in a minute or two, and this tends to destroy something of the illusion of being cut off from the rest of the world. All climbers would welcome the collapse of the great jammed boulders in the gap, which would make this short side 100 vertical feet in height, but no climber would move a finger to engineer this.

But despite the shortcomings of the Rock on this one side, I can think of no more wonderful place upon which to spend a summer's evening than its summit. On many occasions I have perched up there, on a couch of ling or a coil of rope, enjoying all the advantages of being on top of a steeple without having to suffer the snags. Even the controversial conifers 2,000 vertical feet below look almost picturesque from this viewpoint, and one can lazily watch the clouds slowly sailing over miles of distant fells without turning the head.

No sounds reach you on top of the Rock, for you are much too high above the tumbling river and the waterfalls and too remote from the sheep and the occasional slither of scree. Even the chatter of other climbers out of sight and far below is quite inaudible. The only people who can disturb your thoughts are other climbers, who at any moment might appear over the edge, first a hand and then a tousled mop of hair. Climbers are no better and no worse than other people, but they do speak the same language and know, even if they never say so, that the top of the Rock is a place apart.

I have one little regret about the top of the Rock: I've never had my dog up there, although he's been up dozens of ordinary mountains. Dogs have reached the summit, and I think that, with a little effort – and perhaps some help, for he is a big dog – I could get him up there. But perhaps I'll never try. He might destroy someone else's private sanctuary.

THE FAIRFIELD HORSESHOE
30 September 1960

Last Sunday was halfway through before I had recovered from my disappointment at having to abandon, at the last moment, my usual rock climbing day and before I had grown tired of pottering about the garden and worrying whether I'd moved the chrysanths too soon. A walk seemed the next best thing – not too far, since the day was already advanced, but long enough to get the muscles working after a fortnight's idleness. We finally settled, Sambo and I, for the Fairfield Horseshoe, perhaps the most prosaic round in Lakeland.

Fell walking, to the climber, rather tends to be a business reserved for winter and bad weather. We get our walking to and from the crags or at the end of a climbing day but rarely set off in glorious weather just to walk and nothing else. My half-day on Sunday was therefore unusual but, because of this, enjoyable. I missed the crags but found other things in compensation.

Perhaps there is no finer view in southern Lakeland than that from the slopes of Low Pike. There is the whole length of Windermere in the foreground, and on Sunday it was pleasant to sit in the sun and watch the distant motor craft – mercifully silent from this point – making circles like an ice skater on the glass-calm surface. Nearer still, Rydal Water, with its tiny islands and wooded shores, looked so perfect that one could forget the rash of coloured tents that so often spoils the scene in high summer.

The woods under Loughrigg hung upside down in the mirror until a tiny boat put out from the shore and rippled the picture away. South

The Fairfield Horseshoe

of the Coniston fells the sun glinted on a strip of distant, dancing ocean, and 12 miles away, in a straight line to the southeast, I could see the woods on Kendal golf course. All around me the fells, patterned by the slowly moving cloud shadows, lazed in the afternoon sunshine, and a feeling of peace and contentment lay over the countryside.

The magic of southern Lakeland, I decided, as I sat smoking in the sun with Sambo stretched out, panting in the bracken, lies in its woodlands and in its infinite variety of scene. Everywhere there are trees – tiny clusters, little copses or straggling woodlands – and dotted among and around them are the lakes and tarns, with the whole scene hummocked and tilted by the fells. And herein lies the biggest difference between Lakeland and the other mountain areas of Britain: the profusion of our trees and woodlands.

There were only two sounds on this blissful autumn afternoon: the faint murmuring of distant waters and the laughing voices of some young riders jumping their horses over a fence half a mile away on the other side of Scandale.

Over High Pike and Dove Crag we walked and across Hart Crag on to Fairfield. What an extraordinary mountain Fairfield is! Seen from the south, it is a dull grassy hump of fell but, from the north, a long line of high crags, gullies and wild fellside overhanging the solitude of Deepdale. How many people, I wonder, walk around this horseshoe and fail to appreciate the real character of the mountain? I remembered, as we strolled along the summit ridge on Sunday, many long exciting days spent exploring the crags on the Deepdale side when the guidebook to this recently 'discovered' climbing ground was in preparation.

We then feared that when the results of our labours became known the area would become nearly as popular as Langdale or Borrowdale, but Deepdale fortunately still remains a secret valley, and its fine rock climbs are sampled only by the connoisseur.

I looked, too, down the crag where a few years ago two young girls fell to their deaths during a snowstorm and lay undiscovered for weeks, despite the most through searches. Yet to most people Fairfield is a friendly, smiling mountain, easy to ascend and apparently innocent of danger. It is, therefore, amusing to re-read the account of an ascent about a hundred years ago, recalled by Mr Frank Singleton in one of his Lakeland books.

There were four of them in the party, all, I suspect, Cambridge undergraduates, and they had with them 'thirty-six bottles of bitter beer, two bottles of gin, two bottles of sherry, one gallon of water, four loaves of bread, one leg of lamb, one leg of mutton, two fowls, one tongue, half a pound of cigars, four carriage lamps and two packs of playing cards'. They also had a large tent carried on the back of a horse, since they boldly proposed to spend the night upon the slopes, and they carried umbrellas. A gun was fired off at Ambleside when they were seen to have reached the summit, 'and X acknowledged the compliment by tying his pocket handkerchief onto his umbrella and waving it three times' – but surely not expecting his signal to be seen 4 or 5 miles away!

Unfortunately, the expedition came to an inglorious end in the early hours of the morning when the wind blew the tent off its pegs, and the adventurers limped down into Ambleside, bedraggled from the mist and rain, and finished with mountains forever. Whether or not they had by then consumed all of their liquor we are not told, but the story does illustrate the change that has come over our attitude to the mountains in a hundred years.

We completed our circumnavigation of Rydale – surprisingly little visited since it is seen by all travellers approaching Lakeland from the south – by passing over Great Rigg, Heron Pike and Nab Scar and down through the parkland of Rydal Hall to Ambleside. Heron Pike, I have long thought, is possibly a misnomer. It has an Erne Crag on its slopes, and I think that the Ordnance Survey men might have misheard the local pronunciation. An erne is an eagle, a bird much more likely to be associated with the summit in the past than a heron.

Twice we crossed the line of the Thirlmere aqueduct during our walk, once at the beginning of the ascent of Low Pike and again as we came down Nab Scar. The evidence of the existence of the underground watercourse is plain to see at the entrance to Scandale, but perhaps people are not so familiar with its position at Rydal. Here the aqueduct runs through a tunnel cut into the side of Nab Scar. A block of stone carrying no inscription and set alongside the track, above a steep section, marks the position of the tunnel directly beneath.

This is the countryside the Lake Poets knew so well, for Wordsworth lived at the foot of Nab Scar at Rydal Mount and at Dove Cottage and no doubt trod these paths a hundred times. I felt that if he had been with me last Sunday he would have been well pleased, for Wordsworth hated change, and really the scene – in this area at least – is little changed from his day. He would have been pleased that the railway line still finishes at Windermere, and he would not have seen the lake steamers, which he would have hated.

The aqueduct would have puzzled him and would have called for an explanation, and he would have noticed the new houses around Ambleside and Windermere, the increase in the amount of bracken and perhaps the Swaledales instead of the Westmorland Roughs and Herdwicks. But the fells would be otherwise just the same, the tracks a little more noticeable perhaps, but the same distant views, the same familiar woods and Rydal Water – apart from the growing weeds – still apparently unspoiled. It would only be when he got back on the road again and saw the Sunday traffic that he would have really felt upset.

So, in these days of change and speed and noise it is good to know that one can still go for a quiet Sunday afternoon's walk in the hills and see a countryside that has hardly altered in a hundred years. I believe I saw ten people on my modest 10 miles round – one of the most hackneyed fell walks in southern Lakeland – before I rejoined the Kendal traffic queue. Perhaps I had not found anything I had not seen before, but it had certainly not been a wasted afternoon. Just four or five hours alone with the sights and sounds of Nature, with the workaday world forgotten and tomorrow still a long way off.

HELVELLYN
16 June 1961

We are now in the middle of the 'sunrise from Helvellyn' season. Any fine night or early morning at this time of the year – but particularly at weekends – there are quite likely to be people swarming up this great lump of mountain in the darkness, just for the thrill of watching the dawn come up over the Pennines.

There are more impressive mountains in Lakeland than Helvellyn – an uninspiring hump when seen from the main road through the district – but it is easy to understand why it is so popular with the sunrise worshippers. Besides its height – only the Scafells are higher – it is quickly accessible from the road, easily ascended even in the darkness and commands, from its summit, one of the most extensive views in Lakeland. The summit, an unexciting plateau, may have none of the characteristics of a 'real' mountain top, but from it you can see nearly every other mountain in Lakeland and much else besides: the Pennines, for instance, Morecambe Bay, the Solway Firth, several lakes and tarns, and, if you are fortunate, the lowland hills of Scotland.

If you have picked the right sort of morning you will see the eastern sky glowing a rich orange and then gradually change into flaming red. The first golden rim of the sun then shyly peeps over the Pennines and swells into a great ball of fire, and in a few moments it is day and the whole of Lakeland is suddenly flooded with warmth and colour. It is a rewarding sight, well worth the effort, and just the thing to give you an appetite for breakfast. The last time I tried it out I was back home before 7 a.m.

Undoubtedly more people watch the sunrise from Helvellyn than from any other Lake District summit, and I think it is probably true to say that the mountain is climbed more often than any other in England. Indeed, for very many people Helvellyn is their only mountain – their first and last summit. Old men in Preston and Portsmouth will tell you with pride that they went up Helvellyn in 1895, and hundreds of people still remember setting off from, say, Grasmere, for the ascent and reaching the foot of the mountain by four-in-hand. Many have gone up on ponies.

On the summit, particularly on a fine day, you are quite likely to meet people in ordinary town dress or grandfathers or toddlers or young people in fancy hats. I wouldn't be in the least surprised to see a man up there with an umbrella or somebody selling lemonade and postcards.

It's hardly a mountaineer's mountain, and, unlike most of the bigger fells, it has no rock climbing on it whatsoever. I have often thought that a short route might be made on the eastern slopes of the mountain between Striding Edge and Swirral Edge, but it would be a long way to go for just one climb and I can't think of any other possibilities in the area. Even in wintertime the mountain has little in the way of ice-filled gullies to attract the climber, but its ridges can be interesting in severe weather, and it can be a good mountain for the skier.

But principally, I think, Helvellyn is the ideal mountain for the modest walker or the novice. There are at least a dozen routes to the top, and you are not likely to get lost or injured on any of them.

Helvellyn has several interesting or even remarkable features. For instance, it lies halfway along the highest and longest mountain range in Lakeland, but, although it is fairly littered with monuments of one sort and another it contains no real summit cairn. There is the memorial to the dog that lay for weeks beside its dead master, a memorial (on Striding Edge) to a foxhunter and a stone tablet to commemorate the landing of an aeroplane on the summit in 1926. When the aeroplane took off again it flew, after a run of only a few yards, straight over the crags on the eastern side – just above my suggested rock climb – a feat that must have taken considerable courage, whatever one might think about such a publicity-seeking stunt.

Then there is the hidden spring below the summit on the west side of the mountain, the wall shelter near the summit where perhaps one awaits the dawn, and other rather unusual mountain features. But the most remarkable thing about Helvellyn is the complete contrast between its eastern and western sides. Most Lakeland mountains differ in character on opposing sides, largely through weather erosion, but the difference is no more striking than on Helvellyn.

To the west Helvellyn presents an unusually uninteresting side, which completely fails to excite the casual traveller passing over Dunmail Raise. Told that the dreary fellside above him is the famous Helvellyn the average man will probably react in one of two ways: decide it's hardly worth a second glance or decide that he'll run up it the next time he has half an hour to spare. It looks a very easy mountain, particularly from near the summit of Dunmail Raise, but

Striding Edge, Helvellyn

also a very dreary one. No pointed summit, no crags, no wonderful ridge line – just a lot of Christmas trees and, higher up, some grassy slopes. Indeed, it surprises me why people who have only seen this side of Helvellyn ever bother to go up.

But to the east, the Ullswater side, Helvellyn presents a completely different picture and emerges as a mountain of character. Here it is buttressed by fine, lofty ridges, and between the ridges are wild hanging valleys, spattered with crags and waterfalls. The long backbone of the mountain towers darkly over Patterdale and Glenridding and beckons the adventurer to explore its mysteries and its delights.

If you tackle Helvellyn from the west you trudge, with boredom, up unromantic slopes, hoping, perhaps, to catch a sight of a red deer in the plantations to make the effort worth while. Below and behind you is a reservoir, Thirlmere, and even the view of Ullscarf and Armboth Fell across the lake is singularly unattractive. You can probably see buses and chemical containers grinding slowly over the pass.

But from the Ullswater side the fell-walker can be sure of an interesting ascent among fine scenery with lifting views all around him, and something new every corner of the way. In general he can go up the ridges or up the hanging valleys between, or he can switch from one to the other. Most people go up the ridges, and Striding Edge on a summer Sunday can be nearly like a seaside promenade. But the views are better than they are at any seaside, and the interest is maintained to the very top.

Years ago timid walkers fought shy of Striding Edge, but really there's nothing there to daunt even the most nervous. People who don't like heights can avoid the actual roof-tree, but the average youngster will trip along the top without a thought.

I've seen old men of eighty going along there and youngsters of four or five. Except in appalling weather it is difficult to see how anybody could fall over the Edge, unless they jumped off. People have fallen off Striding Edge, but then accidents will happen anywhere. A climbing friend of mine once broke his ankle by falling off a pavement.

A good way to see the sun is to go up one of these edges – Striding Edge, Swirral Edge or the ridge up to Dollywagon Pike or Nethermost Pike – by moonlight and then wait for the dawn on the summit. If you pick the right night you can dispense with torches, provided you keep out of the shadows.

Helvellyn may be the tourists' mountain, but it serves its purpose. No matter what the weather, you can go up there and probably meet somebody else. Perhaps you could call it the friendly mountain.

BLENCATHRA
6 October 1961

As my companion for a day's rock climbing had to call off at the last minute I decided to take the dog for a walk and chose Blencathra and its neighbours, as it seemed a long time since my last visit and on that occasion I remember it was snowing and I was carrying skis. Under certain conditions, particularly when there is snow about, there are few more impressive-looking mountains in Lakeland than Blencathra, although there are at least ten higher.

When you first see the full height of it from somewhere near the Thirlmere dam as you travel north the mountain appears as a great wall of rock, bracken and heather, with its many ridges dropping down to the plains like the flying buttresses of a cathedral. Threlkeld nestles right underneath the wall, and whenever I see this view, particularly when the ridges are etched out by the snow, I am reminded – although on a vastly larger scale – of Innsbruck below the great wall of the Hafelekar.

And if you approach Blencathra along the main road from Penrith the sense of height and bulk is much more impressive than its fewer than 3,000 feet above sea level would lead you to expect. One of the most impressive Lakeland pictures ever taken is the one by W.A. Poucher of Blencathra under snow, with its ridges sweeping down to the valley as if from an Alpine giant.

From all angles – except perhaps from the north – Blencathra looks like a big mountain, and Norman Nicholson has written that if you hollowed it out you would have a dish cover that would fit over London. And, he adds, surprisingly, that all the people alive on the earth could easily be heaped inside it.

The new name of Blencathra is Saddleback, but I prefer the old one. Saddleback is descriptive enough, but the old name has a genuine, rugged ring about it. I don't know what it means, but I don't care. I prefer it to Saddleback in the same way that I prefer Kangchenjunga to Broad Peak or Wedge Peak in the Himalayas.

Blencathra then, is a mountain of character, despite the fact that it is not particularly high and has no crags worth climbing, and the reason is its fine south-facing wall with its array of long, sharp ridges.

Ruskin went up the mountain nearly a hundred years ago by the central ridge to the summit and wrote: 'It is the finest thing I've yet seen, there being several bits of real crag work and a fine view at the top over the great plain of Penrith on one side, and the Cumberland hills, as a chain, on the other. Fine fresh wind blowing and plenty of crows.'

Mr A. Wainwright of Kendal describes this same ridge in one of his guidebooks as 'positively the finest way to any mountain top in the district', but I do not think that I would go so far as that – not enough surprises and changes of scenery   but it is a fine, airy route, nevertheless, straight up the centre of the wall and right to the summit cairn.

From St John's-in-the-Vale it looked a long way, but the dog and I did it on Sunday in just an hour and a quarter from the main road, so it can't have been far. Halfway up we sat down in the heather for three or four minutes for it was warm work although, despite its being October, I was stripped to the waist. Even from 1,500 feet or so the view was very satisfying and marred only by the derelict lead mines and their untidy spoil heaps at the foot of the mountain. I'm glad to know that the unsightly bridge across the road is to be dismantled, but it seems unfortunate that nothing can be done about the derelict mines. Compared with these eyesores, which do not weather like abandoned slate quarries, the railway line looked, from halfway up the fell, completely innocuous and hardly noticeable.

It was interesting, however, to study how Man has brought

beauty to this valley in many ways: the little whitewashed farms and houses, the scattered shelter belts of oak and larch, the cultivated fields inside their irregularly shaped walls and the ragged hedges. And then, as the fields begin to tilt against the side of the fell, the mountain suddenly rears up towards the sky, leaving only the top walls of the last intake fields clinging like a chain below the lower rocks. Green meadows and plough land up to the last walls, and then, suddenly, nothing but the bracken and the heather.

I could see a first glimpse of Derwentwater, but Keswick lay hidden round the corner. Straight ahead rose the great bulk of Clough Head and the Dodds, and the clouds hung low over the Borrowdale fells, but we were in the sunshine and so, too, was the valley below, all the way to Penrith and the Eden. Quickly we pressed on to the summit, up and over the little towers and crags, with Sambo needing a push or a haul here and there but refusing to leave me for the tourist path a little lower down. He was very warm, and his breath was coming out of his gasping mouth like a steam engine.

Blencathra, from St John's Vale

'What a very pleasant, airy mountainside on a bright October morning,' I thought, as we scrambled upwards, and indeed there was much to admire on this ordinary walkers' mountain.

First of all there were the exciting views down into Doddick and Gate Gills on either side of the ridge – splendidly carved combes encircled with crags, floored with bracken turning to russet and here and there a splash of purple heather. And then the sheep, grazing on the terraces among the crags and looking, for all the world, like the kittiwakes perched on the ledges of St Bee's Head. This side of the mountain rises nearly 2,500 feet in a little more than a mile, and for a walkers' mountain there's a grand sense of steepness and space. On either side the ridges sweep downwards, not in jagged lines but in smooth curves, and, if you are very imaginative, you can picture or feel the mountain as some great couchant beast with outstretched flanks and limbs.

And then suddenly you are at the summit cairn and into the wind on a bare, level ridge, and if you take a few steps forward you look over a different world. In a few yards you have stepped off the ladder and are looking out over mile after mile of rolling moorlands – the beautiful, lonely, desolate country known as the Back o' Skiddaw, the country John Peel and his little Galloway knew so well.

We went a long way last Sunday – over Bowscale Fell and round by Carrock and Mungrisdale – but the memories are nearly all of Blencathra, the best of Lakeland's northern peaks. On the summit plateau there are two crosses laid out on the ground, one large and one small. They are shaped out with pieces of quartz and from the air would be unmistakable. I wonder who took the trouble to build them.

Near Sharp Edge we suddenly came upon a pair of ravens, which rose into the wind and hung quivering in the sky until they turned and dropped into the combe like stones, sweeping back again on the wind a moment later, twisting and turning and looping like fighter aircraft. What a magnificent flyer is the raven and how perfectly at home in his mountain fastness of crags and scree.

Before we left for Bowscale I looked back at the summit and saw the steep ladder of Sharp Edge outlined against an angry sky of black clouds, ringed with sunlight and an opening of blue. Hours later, after a bracing day in wind and sunshine, we trotted down through the bracken and saw golden sunlight over Borrowdale and the dark clouds scurrying away towards Penrith. The BBC had been wrong again.

OFF THE BEATEN TRACK
15 June 1962

One of the joys of wandering through the hills of Lakeland or any other mountain country lies in the very pleasant and rather neglected art of following little-used tracks, tracks that the townsman might not even notice.

Fell-walkers do not need to be Red Indian trackers relying on bits of broken twig to help them on their way, but it is all so much more interesting if you have to keep your eyes open. I've known hunters and other hill men who could tell you by feeling the warmth of the hollows in the ground or by observing the way the grass was lying that a fox or a rabbit had just passed that way, but for the ordinary pedestrian this is making things unnecessarily complicated. What I rather have in mind are the instinct for where a track is likely to lie and the ability to follow such a track with ease and confidence, despite the haziest waymarking.

Many of these little-used tracks are not shown on any map nor even indicated in some cases in Mr Wainwright's excellent pictorial guides, but they are almost invariably useful, which is more than can be said for some of the more well-worn and over-cairned popular thoroughfares.

In most cases they have been made by people seeking a shortcut through the fells or an alternative to some over-populated route littered with orange peel. While the 'tracks' to the principal mountain tops become more like highways each year, these little-used trods are the equivalent of the mountain routes of two generations ago. There must be dozens of them in Lakeland, but I am not going to try to compile a list, for they should be sought after and enjoyed.

On Sunday I happened to be on two short sections of track that I last used about twenty years ago. They suggested to me the theme of this article, although they are too well marked to be examples of what I have in mind. One is the track that leads from the col between Coniston Old Man and Dow Crag towards Great How Crags and Swirl How – not the track along the ridge – and the other is the track from Levers Water, through Boulder Valley to the Walna Scar track. Both are obviously fairly well used, but they have not been ruined. They are neither littered nor over-cairned.

But the ideal hill track for the connoisseur in these things is a route that takes the walker easily and surely through difficult country, if he studies the land with care. Ideally, if you are in a hurry, these routes are cairned, but the cairns bear no resemblance whatever to the huge, ugly heaps of boulders that bedevil so many of our Lakeland hill routes. The cairns on these pleasant little trods consist merely of two or three small stones set on a larger boulder, and sometimes even one or two are enough. People unused to these places would never even notice them, but the experienced hill-walker is looking out for them. He cannot see the whole route ahead but, if he uses his eyes, he will spot in front of him perhaps two small stones lying on top of a boulder, and when he reaches this 'cairn' he may be able to see the next. Sometimes the occasional nail scratch will provide further evidence, but in these days of rubber-soled boots there may not be many of these. But most of all he will study the lie of the route, and if he knows his mountains he should find the track where he would expect it to be.

This sort of work through difficult country – craggy, scree-ridden, scored with ravines and generally tumbled – brings a special savour to mountain walking and, at its best, can produce much the same reward that the rock climber enjoys when he is finding his way up unmarked, little-used climbs. We had been rock climbing on Dow Crag on Sunday, but after a time, tired of queuing up on several routes – there were eighteen tents around the rocky shore of Goat's Water – we left early and tried to find a different way home.

But one cannot expect everybody going into the fells to be an expert, and many prefer to keep to well-mapped tracks. Recently

Dow Crag and Goat's Water

discussions have been taking place about the marking of those paths that may not be completely obvious and many suggestions are being considered. My own preference is for a minimum of signposting, and I would prefer that such signs are kept to the roads – simple finger-posts indicating where a mountain road leaves the road and takes to the fells. On the fells themselves I think signposts should be forbidden altogether, but useful signs can often be engraved on boulders. There is one such sign near the start of the Dungeon Ghyll track and another at the foot of Stake Pass. There is no need for a professional job by a stonemason – although the Dungeon Ghyll sign is most expertly done – nor is there any need for letters a foot high crudely scratched on rocky outcrops.

In the Alps they go in for splashes of paint on the rocks – sometimes different colours for different routes – and in Austria some of the paths are handmade, with stone steps and spikes and wire cables to help the timid over the slightly awkward bits. This sort of thing is annoying to the mountaineer, but I must confess that more than once I have been glad to discover the splash of paint for which I had been searching for half an hour.

The last time was a couple of years ago when I was coming down an unknown (to me) glacier after traversing a snow peak. On what should have been an easy way down we got involved in a deeply crevassed area above a steep ice fall. To save time, for the descent would have taken hours, we went back up the glacier, and then one of us spotted a faint splash of red on a crag. It was almost too faint to mean anything at all, but we left the glacier and scrambled round the crag, finding another splash of red, and then another and another until we had worked round the shoulder of the mountain onto the glacier we should have been on all the time. I was glad of those paint splashes then, at the end of a long, hard day, but they are not necessary in the Lake District.

These little-used Lakeland tracks have not come about in a casual sort of way. More often than not they have been deliberately made by some public benefactor who has found a pleasant way round the shoulder of a mountain and has decided to share his discovery with others. Normally, a few tiny cairns have been sufficient to indicate the route to the discerning, and as the way has become increasingly well used the unnecessary cairns are scattered away.

A friend of mine, now dead, was responsible for several of these tracks, one of them being a useful route along the slopes of Langdale Pikes from near the foot of Gimmer Crag to the top of Stake Pass. Another was a route to the top of Coniston Old Man by way of Bursting Stone quarry. One prominent mountain track that was not in existence thirty years ago is that which winds along the ridges of

Glaramara and that is no doubt a product of the holiday hostel at Seatoller.

But the most assiduous track-makers in the Lake District are the mountain sheep, which have been using the same routes across their own heaf for generations and perhaps for hundreds of years. Unfortunately, however, sheep trods are not reliable as a means of descent. They will take you nicely around the contours but rarely downwards. It is quite easy to tell a sheep trod from a human track, for the former is much narrower, never scratched, never cairned and never littered. It also never takes shortcuts and generally keeps as level as possible. But then sheep, despite their alleged stupidity, are level-headed creatures. Unlike many humans on the fells, they know where they are going.

KIRK FELL
25 January 1963

Bulky Kirk Fell, next-door neighbour to the shapely Great Gable, must be one of the most neglected mountains in Lakeland. Although it lies in the very centre of the most celebrated mountain group in England, it is still comparatively untracked, and hardly anybody ever bothers to scramble to its summit – or rather, summits, for there are two of them, half a mile apart and one about 50 feet higher than the other.

If you drive your car to Wasdale Head, the traditional centre for mountaineering in this country, step out at the end of the road and carry on straight ahead on foot you are starting on the ascent of Kirk Fell, for the mountain overshadows the hamlet. But you never see anybody doing this.

When I first used to go to Wasdale Head more than thirty years ago we used to say that the grass tongue of Kirk Fell leading to the inn was the steepest grass in Lakeland, which was probably the reason there were no tracks up there. No doubt there are any number of even steeper grass slopes in the district, but this one seems to be sufficiently tilted to deter the casual walker, so that all the tourist traffic goes past the foot of poor lonely Kirk Fell or round its flank towards Black Sail.

Few of the guidebooks bother to mention Kirk Fell, and my oldest, dated 1916, states simply: 'No track and very steep and slippery. A long grind.' There even seems to be some doubt as to how the name should be spelled, but the Ordnance Survey makes it two words, so I'll stick to this form, instead of the rather more frequently used Kirkfell.

I suppose the principal reason for the neglect of this fine, broad-shouldered lump of mountain is that it is so close to even better things: next door to Great Gable, which some people claim to be the finest mountain in England; immediately facing Scafell and the Pikes, the highest ground in the country; and only separated by Black Sail Pass from Pillar and its great Rock. Small wonder, perhaps, that so many people walk round it on their way to what they believe to be even more delectable heights. And when, to the magnificence of its immediate neighbours, are added the steepness of its rather dull slopes, its comparative lack of feature in the popular Wasdale view, its apparent absence of summit – for it is really a great uplifted plateau – its neglect by the ordinary walker can be understood.

But Kirk Fell is deserving of better treatment than this. It may be a dull hump of a mountain from some sides and it may not have the panache of Great Gable nor the superiority of Scafell, but it is still a worthy mountain – not so high as Gable but twice its bulk, its broad top one of the most wonderful viewpoints in Lakeland, and its little summit tarns providing the perfect upland scene on a warm summer's day. There are a few higher tarns than these in Lakeland, but not many, and there are only a handful of mountains that can boast tarns so near their summit.

These two lie not far short of the 2,500 feet contour and are contained in a hollow between the two summits. They sparkle in the summer sunshine among the mountain grasses and outcrops of pink-grey rock, and if you go up there even on August Monday you will probably be alone with the mountain birds. On the right day the air can be full with the song of skylarks and meadow pipits, and you can dream away the afternoon, sitting in the sunshine and admiring the

Kirk Fell from Green Gable

view. From the tops or the tarns you look out across the Lingmell Beck at the whole long line of the Scafell range notched against the sky, or you can admire the unusual 'side' view of Gable or the switch-back of the Buttermere fells or the sweep of Pillar from Looking Stead.

You can reach this perfect viewpoint from the top of Sty Head by way of Moses' Trod, which runs underneath the Napes ridges or round the 'back' of Gable by Aaron Slack, or by scrambling up from Black Sail Pass. Or you can walk leisurely along the old pony track of Moses' Sledgate from the top of Honister to Beck Head, which is the dip between Gable and Kirk Fell, and thence fairly gently to the top.

But Kirk Fell is not only a walkers' mountain and a pleasant viewpoint, for it is well skirted with crags on its northern side, and these include Boat Howe, a useful climbing ground first pioneered nearly forty years ago. Boat Howe was doubtless so named because it has about it something of the shape of a boat, and its central pillar, called The Boat, is one of the finest pieces of clean, isolated rock in the Lake District.

The pioneers gave the first climbs they made names like Sea Wall Arete, Starboard Chimney, the Hatchway and Rigging, Coastguard Climb and even The Bilge, and years later the impressive Prow of the Boat was first climbed. I remember many happy days on these climbs when it was still possible to spend a quiet summer afternoon far from the queues for the Napes Needle.

Another memory of Kirk Fell is of being lost on the top. It may seem surprising that four experienced mountaineers could be lost in summertime on a modest peak like this, but it happened. We had been climbing on Boat Howe, but at the end of the day, instead of going across to Beck Head and along the Sledgate to Honister, we thought we would first walk over the summit of the mountain. It was misty, but we didn't bother to get out our compasses. After all, we were only on Kirk Fell.

But there are hardly any tracks on Kirk Fell, and what few there are seem to wander all round the mountain instead of across it like sheep trods. We went along one of these, imagining we were steering for the summit, or one of them, but we never reached any summit that day. After about half an hour of not getting anywhere we decided to do something about it, only to find that each one of us had different ideas about where we were. We led in turn, and I suppose during the next hour or so we must have covered most of the mountain. But we found no summit, no tarns, nothing. And maps and compasses were, of course, useless, for we did not know where we were.

I can't remember how long we wandered over the mountain in the mist, but we began to get tired for we had had a long day. We could only see a few yards in the mist and we were feeling hungry too. It was then decided to go straight downhill at the steepest place we could find, thereby getting below the mist but risking a descent into Ennerdale, Mosedale or Wasdale, and after a time the mist suddenly parted and we were looking down on the fields of Wasdale Head. We then had to traverse round the Wasdale side of the mountain and climb all the way up again to Beck Head, so it was four very tired, and humble, mountaineers who eventually trundled down to Honister.

It just shows how easy it is to go wrong on a mountain if you don't look where you are going – even if the mountain is only Kirk Fell.

So this neglected mountain has my respect as well as my affection – a wonderful place from which to survey the best of Lakeland, but a mountain that is perhaps not quite so innocent as it looks.

HIGH STREET
24 May 1963

There's a High Street in nearly every town and village in England – a bustling, crowded highway perhaps, or just the sleepy little road where you find the post office and the grocer's shop – but Lakeland's High Street is nothing like any of these.

How long may be the longest of these tarmacadamed High Streets I cannot say, but the Lakeland one runs for more than a dozen miles along the eastern roof of the National Park, most of it at more than 2,000 feet above sea level, and it has never yet, to the best of my knowledge, been traversed by a motor car. But nearly 2,000 years ago the Romans who built this wild highway in the clouds went along it in their chariots or in slave-borne litters. Centuries later marauding brigands crept along the road, and later still the dalesfolk held horse races up there, accompanied, it is said, by drinking carousals that went on for days.

High Street is the name of the old Roman highway across the fells and also the name of the highest mountain along the range. Fewer than a score of Lakeland mountains are higher. When I first went up High Street as a youngster I used to think it was outside the Lake District. Most of the fells to the east of Kirkstone Pass seemed to us in those days to be remote from Lakeland, and this impression was heightened by the view from the top of High Street of most of our favourite mountains stretched out along the horizon from the northwest to the southwest. And when I began rock climbing the grassy eastern fells did not seem nearly as interesting as the more precipitous places further west.

But as the years went by one found new wonders in these comparatively neglected hills and made the discovery that High Street – the range, not the mountain nor the road – is really an upland of considerable character and charm, with a fascinating history and surprises round every corner. I think it was on High Street, for instance, that I saw my first red deer – the first to be clearly recognised as such – and I certainly saw my first fell ponies up there. The deer, three or four of them, had just climbed out of Riggindale and were silhouetted for a moment on the ridge between High Street and The Knott. They would have made a superb colour picture, sharply outlined against the westering sun, but people didn't take colour pictures in those days. For a few seconds they stood there, poised but relaxed after their climb, and then they must have caught our scent and they were bounding away down the steep slopes towards Hayeswater in a flash.

The fell ponies were grazing in the same area, just below The Knott, wild, shaggy creatures looking much too fierce to be stroked. In those days these might well have been wild fell ponies, but nowadays, although many roam the same fells untended, they are probably in private ownership, perhaps of the lord of the manor.

You need imagination to get the best out of the summit of High Street. If you have none it is just a dull plateau with a survey column stuck on top and pleasant views all around. But it is worth while to sit down for a while and try and picture the ancient Britons who knew these slopes and built their homes and their forts in the surrounding valleys; the Romans marching along the ridge between their garrisons at Ambleside and Brougham; the Scots invaders who fought their way to the top again and again, only to be turned back; and then, in more recent times, the dalesmen at their annual sports. They must have had tremendous energy, these ancestors of ours.

Men from Mardale and Longsleddale and even further afield used to drag barrels of beer and mountains of food up the fellside

High Street

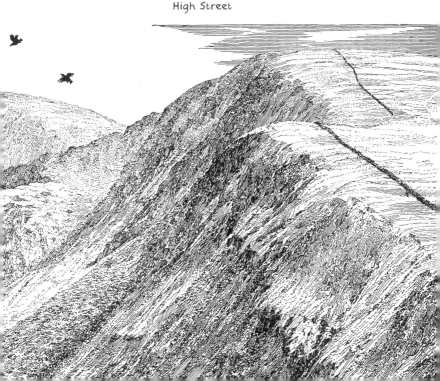

and then race their horses along the grassy ridges or get down to the wrestling. And the Romans, or rather their British and foreign slaves, hauled thousands of tons of rock, much of it sandstone, right up to the ridge and hacked out the road for their horses and chariots. They would drive these chariots, I've no doubt, over the mountains from Carlisle to Galava, which the Norsemen renamed Hamel Saetr and we call Ambleside.

You can still see where the road went and trace out most of its course, all the way from Troutbeck Park, east of Ambleside, to Celleron, south of Penrith. In the Middle Ages Troutbeck Park, now a Herdwick sheep farm, would be a deer preserve, and much earlier still primitive men lived in crude dwellings underneath Ill Bell and Thornthwaite Crag.

The 'road' is only a faint track, which goes up the steep side of Froswick, and today we know this as the Scots Rake, for this is the way the raiders from the north came down from the heights. Once on the ridge you carry on northeast for the summit of High Street, and it is believed that two great stones, lying on the ground, might have marked the way.

The actual summit ridge of High Street is skirted to the west by the Roman road, which then swings eastwards towards High Raise, steering between the crags of Rampsgill Head and Kidsty Pike. This is fine, wild country with steep drops into the surrounding valleys, but armies must have come this way, rounding the crags high up above deep tarns and pressing on remorselessly nor'nor-east for Penrith and the Border.

And after this the way continues, not with so much excitement, over Wether Hill and Loadpot and Moor Divock and on, if you like, to Pooley Bridge and a new county.

There are so many valleys notched into the flanks of the High Street range – Riggindale, Randale Beck, Rampsgill, Measand Beck, Fusedale, Cawdale, Holtondale, Hayeswater and the rest – that the whole area vastly repays careful exploration, but few people go into these coves now that Manchester has made a reservoir of Haweswater and Mardale has become almost a dead valley.

And on the other side of the range there is the deer sanctuary with restricted access so that these quiet, unspoiled dales – once you have turned your back on Haweswater – are among the least visited in the National Park.

The best way up High Street is from Haweswater, and you will probably not meet a soul after you have left your car at the end of the reservoir. You simply climb along the ridge of Rough Crag to the tiny tarn at Gospel Gate and then straight up the pleasant rocks of Long Stile to the summit – a wonderful airy walk with fine views all the time leftwards to Blea Water and right to Riggindale, where you may spot red deer.

I remember taking my dog up this ridge many years ago – not my present dog, but a wild little border terrier named Pip. Soon after we had started he spotted a sheep down in Riggindale and, being a very naughty little dog, set off down the mountain to inspect it more closely. There was nothing much I could do about it, so I carried on, knowing I would have him in full view for the next hour or two if necessary. He went down into Riggindale, chased the sheep nearly into the next valley and then, when he had had enough, climbed up the mountain after me, catching me up when I was eating my sandwiches by Gospel Gate. Here he had to be dealt with, but poor Pip would never learn, having been badly taught before I acquired him.

I simply mention the occasion to illustrate the airiness of the view. Everything below you is in sight, including, of course, the length of Haweswater.

Blea Water, on the other side of Rough Crag, is probably the deepest tarn in Lakeland – certainly more than 200 feet. It was sounded by the Brathay Exploration Group about fourteen years ago, and only two lakes, Windermere and Wastwater, are deeper.

And just over the ridge of Piot Crag is Small Water, one of the loveliest tarns in the Lake District, with the old packhorse track of Nan Bield circling its very edge. I can see the top of the Nan Bield Pass from my window as I write and, just to the left, the beginning of the High Street ridge where the Romans went. It looks quiet and peaceful up there now, but it has not always been so.

SKIDDAW
7 June 1963

The first mountain in the Lake District to be ascended for the view or just for the fun of it was probably Skiddaw. Nobody can be certain about this, but Skiddaw is certainly the easiest 3,000 foot mountain in England, possibly in Britain, to climb, and the early fell-walkers of about 200 years ago found it the least frightening of the Lakeland fells.

The mountain may also be the oldest in the country (our oldest rocks are Skiddaw slates), and even the early mapmakers seemed to know about it. My Robert Morden map of 1680 misses out the Scafells, Helvellyn and most of the other Lakeland mountains but proudly identifies 'Skiddow Hill' and in approximately the correct position, too.

Yet, despite Skiddaw's great antiquity, its excellence as a viewpoint and its association with the very earliest days of mountain walking, many people today write off the mountain as a place of little worth. Because it has no crags for the climber, no exciting ridges and few surprises, and may be ascended with comparative ease by grandmothers and toddlers, too many of us are apt to ignore hoary old Skiddaw. I'm just as guilty as the others.

After my first stroll up the mountain as a youngster – I think we ran all the way down on a very hot day and had to be revived with much lemonade – I left the mountain alone for about twenty years, preferring to seek out more exciting places. I think it is the ease by which the summit may be attained – that, and the ruins of the old refreshment hut emphasising the 'tripper' quality – that mostly puts people off. Mrs Radcliffe rode over the mountain on a pony as long ago as 1794. Bren gun carriers and tanks lurched about its slopes during the war years, and motor cars have, unfortunately, been driven to the summit.

All this is discouraging to the simple walker, and so is the width of the highway that runs some distance up the mountain. But 200 years ago one of the early visitors was so alarmed by the view opening out below his feet that he had to abandon the ascent. Another man found that breathing on the mountain had to be performed 'with a kind of asthmatic oppression' and later, during a thunderstorm, had the unfortunate experience of watching his guide 'lying down on the ground, terrified and amazed'.

So Skiddaw was regarded with some respect many years ago, and, considering that more of England can probably be seen from its slopes than from any other place in the country and its many other virtues, it is a little unfortunate that we value the mountain so little today, for Skiddaw, the fourth highest mountain in England, has many qualities.

As a background to Keswick, it is a noble mountain, the centre of a well-shaped cluster of fells with sweeping buttresses, which seem to emphasise the height of the central peak. The mountain, with its outliers, stands quite alone – save for its proud neighbour, Blencathra – rising steeply from the Keswick plain and the pastures around Bassenthwaite or swelling impressively from its tumbled foothills in the

Bassenthwaite Village and Skiddaw

remote country to the north. This comparative seclusion adds grandeur to the mountain, for its features are rarely hidden by other fells, and Skiddaw looms bulkily in splendid symmetry from most angles.

Admittedly, the easiest way to the top from Keswick may have few excitements, but this is only one of half a dozen different ways up the mountain. Perhaps this was the first tourist route up a Lakeland mountain, and tens of thousands of people have gone this way, but on some of the other tracks to the summit you may never meet a soul. Indeed, although the popular side of Skiddaw may be among the most familiar and least formidable slopes in Lakeland, the 'back' of the mountain is still almost 'undiscovered'. You can find plenty of untracked wastes in the 'Back o' Skiddaw' country that John Peel knew so well and easily get lost there. And the scenery in this little-known part of Lakeland can be invigorating and rewarding – Dash Falls, for instance, and the fine combe of Dead Crags as approached from the road to lonely Skiddaw House.

There can hardly be a more lonely place in England than Skiddaw House, 2 miles due east of the summit of Skiddaw and at least 4 miles across the mountains from any other house. Shepherds live here during most of the year, sheltered by a belt of trees that is the only afforestation in the vast stretch of moorland still called Skiddaw Forest.

The multiplicity of the valleys that skirt Skiddaw and its adjoining fells ensures that the mountain is not one that can be explored in a day or two. Few people can claim to know all these valleys really well, but all of them lead to the summit ridge and each has its own individuality. Indeed, I do not think there is a finer view in the whole of Lakeland than that looking south and west, into Borrowdale and the Lorton fells, from the slopes above Applethwaite or even from the lovely Applethwaite road itself.

Under snow Skiddaw is a wonderfully impressive sight, and it is also one of the most colourful of Lakeland mountains during the summertime and autumn because of the profusion of heather and bracken on its slopes.

In area Skiddaw and its attendant fells are much bigger than the whole of the Scafell range and several times bigger than the Gables, and it is less than 150 feet lower than the highest land in England. It is one of the most shapely and symmetrical mountains in Lakeland, one of the least known (in its northern reaches) and one of the finest viewpoints.

Geologically, it is one of the most significant mountains in Britain, and at most seasons of the year its slopes are among the most colourful. Its crags are not especially striking – Skiddaw slate does not make good climbing rock – but they do at least have the merit of being tucked out of sight of the casual viewer. And yet, despite all these attributes, Skiddaw is a mountain that thousands treat with near contempt.

But what's wrong with Skiddaw? People will tell you its too easy to climb and too near the streets of Keswick. But there are other ways up if you take the trouble to seek them out, and any Keswick resident will tell you, 'It's a grand mountain.'

I think they're right.

CRINKLE CRAGS
26 July 1963

Crinkle Crags is one of the hills I can see from my study window – a blue, knobbly ridge stretched across the sunset and ending abruptly with the northeast corner of Bowfell. If the bumps were a little sharper, I sometimes think, it would not look unlike a section of the Cuillin ridge in Skye, but Crinkle Crags can never attract the fame of this imagined Scottish counterpart and, indeed, has difficulty even in getting into the guidebooks.

This disregard of a fine peak is rather strange, for there are only about twelve mountains in England higher than Crinkle Crags and no other mountain in Lakeland with so many summits – five – while the ridge is as splendid a piece of rock architecture, with crags on either side, as you will find in the northern hills, and there is tremendous scenery all round.

Few Lakeland ridge walks are more impressive than this. All the way along you are stepping on springy turf or firm rock ledges with

Crinkle Crags, from Oxendale

easy stride, the invigorating air seeming to hurry you up and over the rises, and the feeling in your legs that you are covering great tracks of land at incredible speed. It is the rapidly changing views that provide the illusion, a different valley opening up below your feet every few minutes, the Langdale Pikes marching with you on your right and, away to the left, the long line of the Scafells and the highest land in England.

Yet a dozen guidebooks either miss out the Crinkles altogether or dismiss them with a one-line reference as part of a route to Bowfell. An early work tells me, 'very wild and rough', apparently as a deterrent rather than an invitation. And another warns that the walk should not be attempted in bad weather as compasses are liable to go wrong in this area.

Perhaps this exaggerated claim that magnetic rock makes compasses ineffective along this ridge and in the Bowfell area should be briefly analysed. A few years ago a very careful investigation of the phenomenon was carried out when it was found that the only significant variations were in the neighbourhood of Ore Gap, on the other side of Bowfell, where strange readings could be obtained if the compass was placed in actual contact with the rock.

On Crinkle Crags itself there were a few places where minor deviations could be detected, but only if the traveller placed his compass close to the ground. So apparently, if you hold your compass in your hand or on your wrist and use it standing up, as most people do, it should work perfectly well from Pike o' Blisco to Great End. People sometimes find themselves on the wrong side of the ridge in bad weather – in Eskdale, perhaps, instead of in Langdale – not because their compass is playing tricks but simply because the ridge twists and turns so delightfully.

Among the glories of Crinkle Crags are the ravines dipping down into the tumbled recesses of Oxendale or the wild corries of upper Eskdale. These remote combes are among the best places in Lakeland for those seeking impressive, unspoiled scenery, and the agile will be able to scramble up to the ridge by way of nearly a dozen routes, some tracked but most of them unmarked.

Often we've gone up there when the gullies have been filled with snow and the ridge has been reached only by mountaineering approaching the serious. But, even with all this rock about, there's no rock climbing on the Crinkles, the crags proving on closer acquaintance either too loose or too easy and rarely yielding worthwhile continuous routes. Across one or two of them there are curious terraces that may be traversed in safety, provided one is not bombarded by stone falls initiated at the summit. The gaps between the summit crags, as seen from the Langdale side, can sometimes provide good step-cutting practice in wintertime.

Some of the finest tarns in Lakeland lie on or close to the Crinkle Crags ridge. One popular approach to the ridge is from the top of Wrynose Pass, and on the way, underneath Cold Pike, will be found Red Tarn, a quiet, shallow pool wherein dwell several fat trout, and at the far end of the ridge, on the top of the col that separates Bowfell from the Crinkles, lie Three Tarns, with one or two more tiny ones a short distance away. This cluster of tarns must be among the favourites of many who go into the fells. Mostly they are edged by weathered outcrops of light grey-coloured rock so that, in the sunshine, with plenty of blue in the sky and reflections in the water, they make the perfect subject for the colour photographer or painter.

On the ridge itself there are two very small tarns, and more on Shelter Crags (which is really a continuation of the Crinkles, making seven knobs in all). One of the tarns lies quite close to the summit, the highest Crinkle, and even closer to the cairn about 30 yards away is a spring emerging from beneath a boulder. Perhaps this spring is the nearest to any summit in Lakeland.

Prominent in the view from Crinkle Crags today are the cooling towers of the Calder Hall atomic power station, but a much more impressive sight is the long view down Eskdale to the sea and the even finer picture opening out down the 12 miles stretch of Dunnerdale.

For the short day one of the best rounds in Lakeland is up The Band and over Bowfell and the Crinkles, while a longer walk might include the Langdale Pikes and, at the other end, Pike o' Blisco and Cold Pike. During most of this longer walk you are walking along the Cumberland–Westmorland boundary, starting from the Three Shire Stone at the head of Wrynose and keeping on the boundary watershed all the way until you reach the boggy ground at the 'back' of the Langdales.

Sometimes when I have been this way I have diverged a little from the boundary on Cold Pike and traversed along the delightful terrace of Gaitkins and on to Red How and Stonesty Pike. This again is a wonderful, little-visited area, which especially lends itself to photography. The rocky ledges make delightful foregrounds for pictures embracing a wide area of southern Lakeland, and you may spend a day on these slopes and perhaps never meet a soul.

Strange, is it not, that Langdale should be the valley with perhaps the shapeliest mountains in Lakeland stretched all around it, the photogenic Langdale Pikes on the one side and, on the other, the wonderful switchback of Crinkle Crags?

LAKELAND SHOW
23 August 1963

The Lakeland show season is upon us again, and during the next month there will be more people in these parts taking an interest, however perfunctory, in cows than at any other time of the year. Normally, seen over the wall or hedge, they may seem hardly worth a second glance to many of us, but suddenly we realise they come in different colours, some with horns and some without, some incredibly bovine but others quite nice looking and almost intelligent.

Despite our flat caps and tweeds, our muddied brogues and our shooting sticks, we somehow never quite look the part – you simply can't turn a townsman into a countryman overnight. Even those of us who consider ourselves to be countrymen – at least for part of the time – can easily put a foot wrong, confusing an Ayrshire with a Shorthorn, for instance, or showing too much respect for some old bull.

In any event, you can always tell the countrymen, even though they're wearing collars and ties. They look healthier, for a start, and mostly heavier. And they carry sticks for prodding. Indeed, the way a farmer prods a cow and uses his crook on a sheep identifies him right away. If you or I gently prodded a cow it would either ignore us or else swing round, fiercely aggressive. But the farmer, by vigorous prodding in exactly the right place, can achieve just the effect he desires. He can even, with impunity, strike them sharply over the head, telling you they don't really feel it.

The general public look at the cattle in a casual sort of way, reserving their especial interest for the largest and most ferocious looking of the bulls, particularly if they have a ring through their noses. There the cattle stand, beautifully groomed cows, sometimes wearing the red, white and blue rosettes of success on their foreheads, and nearby, looking very bored, the great bulls chained to the fence.

Among them live the white-coated cattle men, quietly scrubbing down an animal's leg or sitting down in the straw eating their lunch. They give the impression that they must almost sleep alongside their charges, and most of them appear to accept cows as reasonably congenial companions. Certainly they can give you the history of every beast and its forebears, and the exact figures of milk yields or the names of champions that have been sired.

You or I may be vaguely interested – if we have nothing better to do – in watching, perhaps, the judging of the bulls, but the farmers are quite prepared to stand round the judging ring for an hour at a time watching a long succession of heavy beasts, male and female, being assessed for their lactation or siring capabilities. They are quite prepared to be severely critical about some apparently flawless prize-winning animal, while on the other hand, any farmer in an official position at the show will tell you that the quality of the stock is the best it has ever been, despite the bad weather or some other phenomenon.

But nobody looks at the poor sheep, except the farmers. They are simply not photogenic enough. To many people, all sheep look more or less alike, except that some have black faces, but to hill farmers the whole business is incredibly fascinating. They are quite happy to spend most of the day around the sheep pens, completely ignoring the cows.

A Grasmere farm

Their untiring interest in Rough Fells, Swaledales, Herdwicks and perhaps Teeswaters, when they see scores of hundreds of them every day of their lives, seems strange. Obviously, there's something about sheep that you or I will never unearth. We would never understand, for instance, why the judges prefer Joe Grisedale's two-shear gimmers to those of Ned Tyson, but to these hillmen it's all just too obvious.

There was a day when the special attractions of the agricultural show for the townsman included the agricultural horses – great, massively legged shires, for example, of stolid, patient mien, looking much too big for any plough and almost too big for work. But those days are now over or nearly so. Now and again two or three might appear, but most of our shows have had to cut these classes altogether, for the whirr and clatter of machinery, even on our hill farms, has replaced the steady plod of these handsome, tireless animals. A pity, for they brought a sturdy old English atmosphere to these shows that the display of shining farm machinery can never achieve.

But it is the horses, the leapers, that keep many of these shows going nowadays – the leaping and the hound trails. Without these attractions some of our shows in the Lakeland area would be hard put to it to draw the crowds. Of course, the Women's Institute marquee (if they have one) can be a big attraction for the womenfolk or even for the men.

There is one show in the Lakeland Country where, among the crowds of country women in the big home industries tent, may also be seen courageous husbands and fathers checking up on whether they have won prizes for orange marmalade or embroidery. And many of them do. One year, indeed, it was a man who won the diploma awarded by a woman's journal for bottled fruit, while men were equally prominent among the biscuits and the squares of gingerbread. Obviously, this onslaught had been appreciated in advance, for the organisers had thrown in a special class, 'any cake made by a man (not iced)'. Here competition was keen, and one had the feeling that the cake-makers could have tackled even an iced cake with confidence, while the winner carried off the medal for the best exhibit in the cookery classes. But it was the 'embroidery in wool' and 'example in basketry' classes that probably put the tin hat on it, for here the only competitors were men, although, chivalrously, they made no challenge with 'knitted socks'.

Generally, our shows are for the farmers in the morning and for the rest of the world in the afternoon. Farmers can even get interested in such classes as 'field of root crops' or 'best-managed arable farm', can then watch and criticise the judging, spend a pleasant hour or so grumbling with their fellows about their hay losses or the weather and then adjourn happily to the beer tent. And another ploy, of course, is to tour the trade exhibits, where liberal hospitality for potential customers is generally dispensed. But the farmers don't waste their time looking at the leaping or the acrobatics on motorcycles and can happily miss the grand parade. Soon they must be back on the farm for the evening milking or even back for the late hay.

But for townsfolk and visitors the day begins with the grand parade, which is the moment when the shows become a public spectacle in place of a farmer's day out. Inevitably, the parade is headed by the largest prize-winning bull on the field – generally led by a pretty farmer's daughter – and tails off towards the end with smaller and less exciting animals, which might include goats. Sheep rarely seem to get a look in. And then comes the leaping, with interest suddenly switched from ponderous, slow-witted beasts to bright little girls in jodhpurs and jockey caps.

There may be a seeping away of interest while the hound trails are run off, but with these out of the way and the possibilities of the trade stands completely exhausted and the third sitting of lunch at an end and a rumour that the refreshment tent has run out of beer, all that remains to be done is to sit back and watch the hunters. It may not be up to BBC television standard and the fences don't look very high, but it makes a nice change.

And then the loud speaker repeats for the fourth time: 'Will the owner of the little boy in the blue suit please collect him at the secretary's office?'

Most of the cattle and sheep are out of the way by now, and long evening shadows are beginning to creep across the show field. Soon it will be all over – the end of just another show day in the fell country.

CHRISTMAS MEMORIES
18 December 1964

It's too early yet to guess with any accuracy the sort of weather we are likely to get over Christmas in the fell country. Writing from ten days away it seems we could have snow, ice or more flooding or perhaps just a mild, misty day with strangely quietened roads, the lights on all day in the houses down the valley and the fells asleep and unseen in the murk. And so I have been casting my mind back among many other Christmases – a few of them in the jungle or desert, and one or two in brightly lit cities, but all the rest in and around the Lake District.

There are childhood memories of short walks along frosted lanes for the exchange of presents or of going off, combed, washed and best-suited, by taxi to a Christmas party, and many, many pictures of Boxing Day expeditions into the hills or through snow-laded woods. And the bandsmen standing in the snow, playing 'Christians Awake' on Christmas morning or one's return from a walk, with reddened cheeks and new gloves or scarf, to roaring fires, roast pork and stuffing, mince pies and carols around the piano.

Out of all these Christmas memories three outdoor days can be recalled in detail. The rather blurred overall picture of all the other Christmases is of rather foggy, windless days with only a few hours of daylight, the curtains drawn from after lunch, only an occasional motor car, its lights peering through the gloom, moving up the valley, the lakes calm and hung with mist and a great stillness over the land. But these three days were different. On one of them we were struggling through the deepest snow I can ever remember in the Lakeland hills, on the second we ate our Christmas dinner in the sunshine by the side of a frozen tarn, and on the third we enjoyed the sort of outdoor winter's day that one remembers when all the wet and miserable days have been forgotten.

The snow adventure was more than thirty years ago, and I cannot now remember whether it was Christmas Day or Boxing Day. We set off, four or five lads, to walk up Coniston Old Man for the fun of it, and not far above the village we were up to our knees in the snow.

The boat landings, Derwentwater

All the paths had disappeared, and a furious wind was whipping the snow into tremendous drifts. It was also snowing hard, and there were times, later on, when hail or bits of ice hurled across the mountain by the wind struck into our cheeks and brought pricks of blood that dropped onto the snow.

The crags on the approach to Low Water were sheeted in ice and hung with icicles yards long, and the tarn itself was a piled jumble of ice floes, dimly seen through the blizzard and looking like some remote corner of the Arctic. Here, we took stock of the situation, for every feature of the mountain was completely covered in the snow and visibility was down to only a few yards. But we were fit and young, well used to the mountains and, for those days, well equipped. There were no anoraks or proper windproof garments at that time, but we were smothered in warm clothing, scarves, woollies, goggles and the rest, wore good nailed boots and carried ice axes and ropes. We decided to carry on.

One of the party took the lead, and we steered a compass course for the unseen summit – the first and only occasion I have used a compass on Coniston Old Man, which I have climbed scores of times.

On our way to the top we stumbled on what proved to be the roof of a quarry hut and managed to drop inside through a broken window or skylight. This was the only shelter we found – and this was purely by accident – and we ate our sandwiches inside this dark hole completely sealed in by the snow. Getting out through the roof again proved awkward, but we finally managed it, and our compass bearing took us up very steep slopes, where we kicked and cut steps to the summit.

In those days the cairn on the top of Coniston Old Man was about 12 feet high, but on that Christmas thirty years ago it was completely buried in the snow, and the summit of the mountain was smooth and unmarked. I remember one of the party removed his goggles and glasses on the top to wipe his eyes, but the wind was so furious that he couldn't get his glasses on again and he had to be led, blinded, down to the shelter of Goat's Hause before he could put them on. And when we got down to our hut in the valley we took off our frozen clothes, which looked and felt like armour made out of ice, and stood them up in a corner.

I have never known more severe weather conditions on the Lakeland hills, but we enjoyed every minute of the adventure. A photograph taken on our return made us look as if we had just returned from the North Pole.

The second memorable outdoor Christmas Day was ten or twelve years ago – a perfect winter's day of hard frost, bright sunshine and tremendous Alpine views. The only sounds in a white, silent world were the distant cries of the village children tobogganing in the fields down by the river.

We drove along crackling snow ruts, up the long winding gill and, on the edge of the fells, snapped on our skis. The snow, just deep enough to cover the tussocks of heather and nicely crusted, sparkled as we slid noiselessly down the fellside, and a handful of sheep, nosing through the drifts for the grass, hardly bothered even to look up as we skimmed past. We felt sorry for the sad bundles of wool, their noses topped with chunks of snow from their burrowing, for underneath the snow the ground was rock hard.

By the time we were back at the top again for a second run the late afternoon sun had sunk well down towards the sea, making the whole of the western sky a bright backcloth of gold flecked with dusty grey clouds like oversize gun bursts. The estuary, many miles away, danced in the distant sunshine, and behind us the great fells stood deeply plastered in snow so thick that even the crags were hidden.

A pair of whooper swans, visitors from Iceland looking for a winter home, sailed low over the slopes, and a little field mouse crept out of a hole in the snow and went exploring. A late glint of sunlight caught and burnished the rich colours of an old stone barn, and the stately old larches idly flicked the snow from their fingertips. And half an hour later a fine half moon, with a single star at her foot for company, shone out on a crisp white world as we drove back along frosted roads towards a warm fire, a welcome drink and a slap-up Christmas dinner. How much better it tasted than if we'd been lazing in front of the fire all day.

But three years ago we ate our Christmas dinner – or at least some pork sandwiches and mince pies washed down with a bottle of wine – seated, with our skates on by Tarn Hows.

There has not within my memory been such a perfect outdoor turn of the year in the Lake country as there was that year, for you may remember there was skating over Christmas, skiing over New Year and something like a fortnight of long sunny days. And it was not the usual English snow and ice, either wet and sloppy or wrinkled and blotchy, but instead smooth black ice calling for the sharpest blades and the sort of perfect powder snow we pray for in Switzerland. For days, almost weeks, the skies remained remarkably clear, with superb views, while the sun was strong enough at times – if you picked your spot – to get yourself sunburned.

The Christmas Day skating on Tarn Hows was perfect. We found a little bay, sheltered from the slight breeze by the trees, and ate our Christmas dinner (we had a second one in the evening) while lolling in the sunshine at the side of the ice. And then back to the skating in shirt and sweater – the sun was too warm for a jacket – until the sun went down and the stars came out.

We watched the fells that encircle these superbly situated pools turn purple towards evening, the western sky behind them glow orange and then flame with gold, and then a great, frosty silence came down and gripped the earth in its fist until the bright sunlight of the morning. That, indeed, was a memorable Christmas Day.

As this will be the last time these notes appear this year, may I wish all my readers an equally good Christmas – if possible an outdoor one – and a happy and prosperous New Year.

SCAFELL PIKE
2 July 1965

It has been written that the discovery of the Lake District may be said to have been completed when William Wordsworth climbed to the top of Scafell Pike on 7 October 1818. Samuel Taylor Coleridge had been up sixteen years earlier, but not many tourists before Wordsworth had thought it worth while to scramble to the highest point in England. Indeed, the mountain was not even named in those days, although a few years later it was stated that the shepherds knew it as 'the Pikes near Scafell'.

In the intervening century and a half the shape of Scafell hasn't altered a great deal, apart from the addition of its huge ugly cairn and the Ordnance Survey triangulation column, but the mountain has become a Mecca for thousands of weary pilgrims each year, just because it happens to be higher than anywhere else.

The views are just as good, if not better, from some other Lakeland mountains, but while hardly anybody bothers to go to the top of Broad Crag or Ill Crag, less than half a mile away and nearly as high, the rocky track to the Pike becomes almost a crowded highway on most summer weekends. Nearly every scrap of grass and vegetation has been kicked and trodden off the top – they say the dwarf willow used to grow up there, but I've never found it – and the tracks have been scratched into white highways across the grey wilderness of rocks.

Litter abounds on the worst days, and gangs of scouts and voluntary wardens have to go up regularly to do other people's scavenging. So the summit is not an especially attractive place, and even less so when it's crowded. Many indignities have been perpetrated on top, things that nobody would dream of doing on the summit of Scafell, the climbers' mountain. Beacon and bonfire lightings, flag flyings, tablet unveilings and services and meetings of many kinds may be excused, but the dragging to the summit and the dumping there of an old iron bedstead was deplorable.

And the strange thing about Scafell Pike is that although thousands go up there every year and the tracks across its top are the easiest to follow in the district, the mountain is, in some ways, almost a secret mountain. It is hidden from many parts of Lakeland by its neighbours, and on some of the ascents the summit is masked for most of the way. Its shape is not nearly as recognisable as those of many much lower Lakeland summits, and, as often as not, the mountain is seen more as a wrinkle on a ridge than the highest point in the country.

And while people are going up and down its tracks almost every day of the year, very few bother to explore the mountain, especially its wild eastern slopes, so you cannot say the mountain is really well known, for almost all the visitors stick to the main highways. And the reason for this is that Scafell Pike, because of its accident of height rather than its splendours, attracts every type of walker, including the least experienced, and many of these visitors find the going tough enough on the ordinary paths without bothering to go exploring. For this is undoubtedly the roughest, rockiest country in England as well as the highest.

The mountain is girt with crags on all sides, its summit heaped with boulders and its slopes strewn with screes, so that although all the tourist ascents are easy they are all long and slow, for you can't trip up and down Scafell Pike anything like so quickly as you can Helvellyn.

The real rewards of Scafell Pike, therefore, are away from the tourist routes and the litter. How many of the thousands who haul themselves to the top, for instance, know Broad Crag Tarn, perhaps a quarter of a

The Scafells, from Crinkle Crags

mile southwest of the summit, but some distance away from the usual track? This is the highest tarn in Lakeland, 2,746 feet above sea level, an impressive little pool lying in a solid rock basin not far from the ridge of Mickledore and the dark overhangs of East Buttress.

The smallest tarn in Lakeland – and the second highest one – is Foxes Tarn, on Scafell, just across the rocky scramble out of Eskdale to the Mickledore gap.

And how many Scafell Pike visitors have seen the great precipices of Dow Crag, low down on the Eskdale side of the summit, one of the steepest crags in Lakeland and known to climbers as Esk Buttress? Or have walked across to the fine pinnacle of Pulpit Rock overlooking Hollow Stones, the finest viewpoint for Scafell Crag, the most remarkable cliff in England? Or have walked from the upper Esk into Little Narrowcove and thence up to the summit ridge through almost untracked country? Once during a climbing expedition to Esk Buttress we watched shepherds from Brotherilkeld Farm winkling out fox cubs from a borran right underneath the crag.

I've climbed in late evening sunshine up the walls and chimneys of Pikes Crag when the other crags were shadowed and quiet and walked across Mickledore after a night on Scafell when, with the dawn, we had seen not only the Isle of Man but also Slieve Donard in County Down, 100 miles away.

Scafell Pike, then, may be the king of English mountains but you have to get to know it to appreciate this.

The walk up from Wasdale by Hollow Stones or from Borrowdale by the Corridor Route or from Langdale from Esk Hause will not really teach you a lot about this great sprawling mountain. Too many inexperienced people do this every year in poor equipment or in bad weather and get back merely exhausted and perhaps fed up with the mountains. And some have died because they underestimated the size of the mountain and its savagery in storm or in the wintertime, while many school parties, ill led, have been lucky to get down unscathed.

There's more to learn about the Scafell range than any other mountain group in the country, and yet, off the tracks, it is relatively little known. Its potential dangers for the inexperienced tourist are greater than anywhere else in Lakeland. It is, for instance, the only mountain ridge that cannot be traversed by the ordinary walker, who, to avoid the rock climb of Broad Stand, has to make a wide detour to go from the Pike to Scafell. Immediately below the tourist path of the Corridor Route there is the tremendous ravine of Piers Gill, which can be a death trap for the unwary and indeed is negotiable only by climbers during periods of exceptionally dry weather. And on the other side of the mountain, overlooking the upper Esk, there is the wildest and roughest country in Lakeland.

But the youngsters in low shoes who set off each summer weekend to climb to the highest point in England don't know these things, and that's why we have the accidents and the mountain searches. The real Scafell Pike is not a tourists' mountain but a mountain to be studied over many visits and in all weather until its secrets have been learned.

The name Scafell Pike is really an inaccuracy, and the Ordnance Survey's 'Scafell Pikes' is probably more accurate. Actually, the peak is 'the Pikes near Scafell', for the name is properly applied to its slightly lower but even grander neighbour. 'Scawfell' had crept into some guides and maps (and hotel names) because of the pronunciation. The accent, of course, should be on the first syllable, as in nearly all Lakeland place names: KESwick, PENrith, BOWness, LOUGHrigg and so on.

But the derivation is 'sca' (or scar, scaur or scarth, a Norse word meaning steep or sheer), the word 'scaw' being meaningless. The shepherd says 'Scarf'l' or something like it, but if you pronounce the name of the highest mountain 'Scawf'l Pike' (although writing it Scafell Pike) you won't be far wrong.

FRIENDLY GIANTS
20 August 1965

When high summer comes to Lakeland, as it did last week, you could hardly enjoy it better than striding along the lazy switchback of fells that overlook the shores of Buttermere. Perhaps there are no more enchanting hills than these in Lakeland. They have their great crags, their lonely tarns, their splendid waterfalls and their magnificent views of the cluster of unspoiled lakes far below stretching out towards the Cumberland plain. And you walk on springy turf along the swinging ridge line, with the views changing every five minutes, so that you seem to be covering the ground at great speed.

I always loosely call these delectable little hills the Buttermere Fells, although the Ordnance Survey apply the comprehensive term Buttermere Fell to the southwestern slopes of Dale Head, Hindscarth and Robinson on the opposite side of the valley. But to me these fells with their long combes sloping down towards Keswick more rightly belong to the Derwent, while the real Buttermere Fells, in my view, are those that so splendidly circle the head of the dale, show their high corries to the lake and send down their streams and waterfalls to the valley.

The Buttermere Fells, from Mellbreak

This is the best side of these hills – the Buttermere side – and to me, rightly or wrongly, they will always be the Buttermere Fells. I include among them the trinity of shapely summits known as High Crag, High Stile and Red Pike, with their attendant guardians of Haystacks, often dark and menacing, and the quarry-scarred precipice of Fleetwith Pike.

Perhaps I visit them most of all for the rock climbing on clean, airy cliffs that dry quickly in the sunshine, but as walking country they are almost unsurpassed. Being slightly removed from the more popular holiday centres these fells are often quiet and never crowded so that the birds and wildlife are little disturbed. There always seems to be something to see once you are up on the ridge: the bulk of Pillar Rock seen across the Liza and the dark carpet of conifers creeping up Ennerdale; the sunlit crags in the high corries; a white sail, perhaps, on Buttermere or Crummock; the 'backside' of Gable and its outliers; the remarkable profile of Honister Crag; the savage recesses in the Haystacks; magical upland pools like Blackbeck Tarn; and some of the best waterfalls in Lakeland.

Always these will be friendly fells. You can be in the sunshine all day long and take your time, and I've even gone to sleep between pitches on the climbs, curled up on a grassy ledge, with the steep drop below, the blue lake beyond the combe, white wisps of cloud overhead and nothing else in sight. Even high up on the crags you can smell the thyme on the corrie floor or lie on a couch of bilberries, idly eating the purple fruit.

Not far below you the insects are whirring in the scorched grass, the Herdwicks slowly seeking out the more succulent grazing between the boulders and the becks sliding and trickling down the fellside. There are no better places for the lone camper in the whole of Lakeland than in these lonely, rock-girt combes, no better recipe for getting away from it all than to wander along these quiet heights or to climb the grey crags that soar towards the summits.

I think the late Professor W.G. Collingwood exactly caught the feeling of this lovely valley and its encircling hills when he wrote: 'But I always think of this valley as made by Heaven for summer evenings and summer mornings; green floor and purple heights with the sounds of waters under the sunset, or lit with the low northeastern sun into pure colour above, and the greyness of the dew upon the grass.'

This sort of scene is the reward of the camper when he opens his tent flap beside one of the becks underneath High Stile on a summer morning or takes his last look at the hills before turning in for the night.

There are few more satisfying walks in Lakeland than the ascent of Fleetwith Pike from Gatesgarth, the round of the chain as far as Scale Force and then the easy walk down to Buttermere. Or you can, if you like, continue over Starling Dodd and Great Borne and on to Herdus End overlooking Ennerdale Water, which are properly part of the same chain. Haystacks, which should be part of the round, is a fascinating mountain – a huddle of rocky tors with jewelled tarns set among the crags and winding crags, which, on a misty day, seem to be leading nowhere.

Between these jumbled hummocks, drained by dark vegetatious gullies, and the 'backside' of Fleetwith is the splendid pit of

Warnscale Bottom, threaded by a steep path through the screes and guarded by Striddle Crag, a new climbers' playground. The ancient pass of Scarth Gap lies between Haystacks and the steep gable end of High Crag, but once on the ridge there is airy walking all the way to Scale Force. In turn, one passes above the saucer-shaped corries of Birkness Combe, Bleaberry Combe and Ling Combe with the well-shaped peaks of High Stile and Red Pike in between. Down on one's right are the turreted crags and the scalloped ridge and, to the left in great contrast, a wooded fellside sloping down to Ennerdale.

From Red Pike you can run down over The Saddle and down to the meadows below Sour Milk Ghyll – a quick and exhilarating descent – rounding Bleaberry Tarn on the way. Red Pike looks red because of its pink Ennerdale granite, and the bed of the tarn was scoured out by ice and not by a volcano as some people once thought.

But if Scale Force, one of the biggest cataracts in Lakeland, is to be visited it is necessary to keep along the ridge, and here the scenery suddenly changes. One minute you are trotting along a ridge pole with fascinating downward views on either side; the next you are in rather dreary moorland country. But the outward views towards the great Cumberland plain, with the lakes still stretched out below, continue.

The walk along the ridge in the reverse direction is perhaps even more satisfying, for then you have the big central fells just in front of you. From the top of Red Pike you can look across at the crags and buttresses of Kirk Fell and Gable and pick out, through a gap between them, the great northern precipice of Scafell.

Buttermere has always been among my favourite Lakeland valleys – a quiet place except at springtime when the whole valley seems noisy with the sound of sheep and their lambs. If you are approaching the valley for the first time come in from the northern plains and so watch the gradual unfolding of one of the most restful scenes in England. Notice how the scenery changes from the pastoral to the colourful and then, through impressiveness and grandeur, to the windiness of its magnificent valley head. The dale – once Nicholas Size's *Secret Valley* – is still as unspoiled as anywhere in England, and, with its hostels, huts and camping grounds, is essentially a place for the young in heart. And its surrounding heights are unmatched for beauty and symmetry – a noble, exciting but friendly skyline for those with the youth and vigour to enjoy it.

THE SWITCHBACK SKYLINE
3 September 1965

The best ridge walk in eastern Lakeland and one of the neatest progressions of little hills in the country is the switchback skyline you see on your right as you climb up Kirkstone Pass from Windermere. These shapely hills begin beyond Garburn Pass, which winds over the commons from Troutbeck to Kentmere, and continue due north towards High Street.

We call them Yoke, Ill Bell, Froswick and Thornthwaite Crag, and they have no collective name so far as I know, although we always call them the Troutbeck Fells. The Romans knew these hills well for they went with their packhorses up the hillside from Troutbeck to the northern end of the little ridge and then northeast over High Street and Loadpot Hill to the outskirts of Penrith. You can still trace their route up Hagg Hill, and then by way of what we now know as the Scots Rake on to the ridge; thereafter, along High Street, the way is plain to see.

I can see the Troutbeck hills end-on from my house. First, the great bulk of Yoke with the black precipice of Rainsborrow Crag dropping down into Kentmere, then the shapely cone of Ill Bell behind and, a little to the east, the summit of Thornthwaite Crag, with its 14 foot high beacon clearly visible on the best days.

The best-known view of these fells, however, is that from the Kirkstone road, where you can see them from top to toe – smooth, grassy slopes dropping steeply to the Trout Beck with the ridge itself, especially under snow, looking like a brown sail against the sky. But from the opposite side of the ridge, the Kentmere side, the view is even more dramatic, for here the steep slopes break into crags that look dark and savage against the westering sun. It is the usual feature of a Lakeland ridge: smooth slopes on one side and on the other, the northern or eastern side, the fellside carved into combes and hanging valleys with crags and buttresses in between.

Ill Bell, perhaps the best known of these hills, is one of the most graceful and beautifully shaped fells in Lakeland. From certain angles it really is shaped exactly like a bell, symmetrical and rounded, and this is almost certainly the derivation of the name. But Ill has nothing to do with hill, although the mountain is called Hill Bell on the 2½ inch Ordnance Survey map and was so named in the guidebooks of a hundred years ago. It is suggested that Ill, in this case, is the same as Eel, which is said to be a derivative of E'il or evil. You can find the same word in several parts of Lakeland – Eel Tarn, Eel Crags, Ill Crag and so on – all of them, supposedly, dark and foreboding places, although I have never found them so.

But one of the most interesting features of Ill Bell is its multitude of summit cairns. I've never counted them, but there must be half a dozen quite large ones and several smaller ones as well. They are scattered right across the summit, so that, in mist, you are always stumbling into them without knowing exactly where you are, but their presence, although often a nuisance, gives the mountain a distinctive appearance when seen from afar. From Dove Crag, Fairfield or Red Screes, for instance, the cairns look like the crumbled remains of towers, and when you spot them from these or several other tops you know immediately you are looking at Ill Bell, for no other Lakeland summit has this characteristic.

Why they were built in such profusion on a modest summit less than 2,500 feet high I cannot guess, but they are quite fine specimens of their kind and immeasurably superior to the ugly heaps that litter the approaches to Gable and Scafell.

Less than 2 miles away to the northeast is another Ill Bell, Mardale Ill Bell, set on a spur of High Street that looks down on Blea Water and Small Water. It is strange there should be two hills of the same name so close to each other, for they have little in common. Mardale Ill Bell is not much more than an outlier of High Street, except on its northeastern side, where it has several dramatic features. You may see red deer and fell ponies on Mardale Ill Bell, but you are unlikely to do so on the Troutbeck fell.

Froswick is almost an exact replica of Ill Bell, although a little smaller, while Yoke is rather a dull mountain except on its Kentmere side, where it is a mass of crag that has never produced any rock climbing worthy of the name because of its looseness but is a rare place for foxes.

Most people go on to Ill Bell by way of Yoke and continue the walk northwards towards High Street. Another easy approach is by the Scots Rake. Thornthwaite Crag, which overlooks four valleys, is a fine viewpoint, and, as the summit is readily seen from many directions, it has long been a beacon. The column on the summit is one of the most remarkable cairns in Lakeland, well built and climbable by the agile.

From both Thornthwaite Crag and Ill Bell very fine views of southern Lakeland, including the long length of Windermere, may be seen. Perhaps it is best to approach the ridge from the north so that this pleasant prospect is always ahead of you once you have reached the top.

The Ill Bell range

The Romans would see the view from their high road to the northeast, but perhaps they weren't interested in scenery, but only in getting across a wild, foreign land as quickly as possible. They wore the grooves up the side of Ill Bell with their traffic, and their way across the plateau to High Street, which must have been difficult in mist, was marked by two great stones, which you can still see to this day.

Then across the broad backbone we still call High Street, with steep drops to Blea Water and Riggindale on their right and Hayeswater far below to the left, and on to the sharp peak of Kidsty Pike went the road that makes such exhilarating walking today. And on to High Raise and Red Crag and Wether Hill and eventually to Moor Divock, where you may see sepulchral cairns, and so to the toe of Ullswater and the Eden plain.

All this starts in the Troutbeck hills, in the valley that was once a deer park. They are easy, accommodating hills – a motor cyclist has traversed much of their length – but to walk along them in autumn when the colours are changing and the distant views are sharp and inviting is one of the best things to do with a day based on Windermere or Ambleside.

QUIETLY INTO AUTUMN
5 November 1965

Lakeland seemed to stumble, almost overnight, into winter last weekend and then, surprisingly, a couple of days later slide back into autumn again. One day we were still enjoying the loveliest October for years, and the next – or so it seemed – we were battling with gale-force winds, flooded roads, hail storms on the tops and even the threat of snow. Indeed, it was snowing further north. And then, by Tuesday morning we were suddenly back in autumn again, but the back end of autumn now, with most of the trees stripped of their leaves and a new bite in the air.

If it had not been for Nature's violent fling right at the end of the month, October would probably have been a record month in

Lakeland – a record for sunshine and absence of rain. Until the weekend storms Langdale, often one of the wettest places in England, had had just 3 inches of rain in October, about one-quarter of its usual ration for the month. And even counting the two very wet days right at the end of the month, the total was only about one half of normal.

October is often one of the best months of the year in Lakeland – dry, sunny and colourful – and this is the direction in which the season is likely to extend. Almost every day last month those of us fortunate enough to live in the area awakened to still, hazy mornings that blazoned, an hour or two later, into days of glorious sunshine and unbroken blue skies. The great winds that can sometimes sweep the leaves from the trees almost overnight spared us for almost the whole month. Instead, we had the gold and russet carpet falling daintily, a little more each day, and the trees moved quietly into autumn with grace and dignity.

The ash, often the latest to come into full leaf, was the first to fall, but the oak and the beech stood firm, the foliage growing richer every day. Even today, after one of their worst batterings for years, the oaks around my house are still thickly clothed, while the ash is bare and brown against the sky.

Never has there been a finer pageant of colour in the woods, along the roadsides and across the bracken-covered fellsides than this autumn, and often the lakes have mirrored the picture to perfection. One day we came down from St Sunday Crag and saw the length of Ullswater stretching out towards the distant meadows around Pooley Bridge, the lake shining in the late afternoon sunlight like a scimitar curved around the flank of Place Fell and its three tiny islands like toys on a sheet of glass. Down through the steep woodlands we came, along a rustling carpet of leaves, and through a gap in the larches we looked across the Grisedale Beck at Lanty's Tarn on its little ledge above the lake. There's an old wood of ragged Scots firs beside the tarn, and even at that distance we could see the trees exactly mirrored in the tiny pool.

Down in the valley the dogs were barking at Grassthwaite How and the rattling of pails came up the fellside. But there were no other

Ullswater, from St Sunday Crag

sounds, and the smoke from the cottage chimneys in Patterdale rose
slowly and straight to the sky. How different the picture a few days
later, with yachts and small craft on Windermere swamped and driven
onto the shores and the wind strong enough on the Coniston fells to
fling a party of youths through the air and put one of them in
hospital!

Morning after morning during October I watched the great red
orb of the sun rise slowly from behind Benson Knott and gradually
melt away the mists that cloaked the fells until they emerged, first in
hazy outline and then in sharp focus. Elsewhere they had fog, but not
in Westmorland. It's a gradual process, this preparation for the long
winter, even though the magic sometimes comes overnight. We wake
up some sunny morning, before the gales have blown all the leaves
away, to discover that the picture has been repainted while we slept
from the other side of the palette – the warm colours of brown,
yellow, orange and red in place of the familiar green. There's a new

smell of woodsmoke in the air from the cottage fires, and the weekend gardeners and enterprising small boys begin hauling bonfire material across the fields and along the lanes.

There was a time when the fell country went into its long winter sleep about this time of the year – the last holidaymakers departed, the traffic stilled, the hotels closed, the lake steamers moored for overhaul, and the village streets deserted – but those days are now gone. For the traffic remains, with a new purposeful hustle everywhere, and a sunny weekend still brings out the trippers in their thousands. The farmer, perhaps, with his fields ploughed, his fences clipped and soon his cattle inside, can take things a little easier, and the boatmen can get on with their painting, but the forester will be busier than ever, and most bright mornings the hunters are away to the fells.

November brings the shepherds' meets and probably the first snows in the hills, and, indeed, there were patches on Bowfell this week. The month can also bring the fog, although Lakeland generally escapes the worst of it, and sometimes there are September days when the whole of the Lake District is bathed in sunlight, but the 10 mile trough of Windermere, the longest lake in England, is completely filled with fog. From above, the effect is remarkable – blue skies and sunshine all around, but the valley completely shrouded in off-white cotton wool, with here and there the tip of a mast just peeping through.

Sometimes the Windermere morning fog has coincided with the annual overhaul of the ferry that hauls itself across the lake on chains, and passengers have had to be taken across the 600 yards of water in an ordinary motor launch. A few years ago the launch managed to get itself lost in the fog several times – once it nearly ran into Belle Isle – and there were delays of up to an hour with the ferry going round in circles until somebody thought of taking a compass on board.

Shepherds' meets are jolly affairs. Perhaps there was a time when they were more serious, a businesslike arrangement for the exchange of stray sheep found on the fells during the year, but not in my memory. Really, I suppose, they are just an excuse for a 'reet good do', and the sorrowful-looking strays play only a minor part. The shepherds drive them in over the passes or bring them along in the back of a van, and they are cooped in a pen and left, tightly packed and steaming, while the men get down to the serious business of following the hounds or propping up the bar. Perhaps those interested may take a look at the sheep later on and see if any of the mixed bag belong to them, but there's no hurry, and anyway the old shepherd in charge can be well trusted to sort them out.

The main object in the morning is to get out after the hounds or the harriers, and after that there's the 'tatie-pot' dinner, with plenty of pickles and apple pie and cheese to follow, and the rollicking singing of the old hunting choruses that will go on until the landlord calls 'Time'. They say the jollity used to go on for three days until everybody was exhausted, but shepherds are not like that now, and it was all a long time ago.

HIGH SUMMER
22 June 1968

High summer, with shade temperatures nudging the eighties, came to Lakeland this month – a little soon, but very welcome – and the forecasters are already talking about a long, hot season.

As I write, earlier in the week, a drowsy heat haze hangs over the fells and the music of a thousand becks is stilled. The grass is turning brown, but here and there the bright fronds of the new bracken show freshly green. The lakes are lower than they have been for months, and some days hardly a ripple has stirred on the waters. And you can watch for half an hour in the soft cool of the evening without seeing a fish rise.

Up on the crags at the weekend we have felt the heat rebound from the great rocks like sound from a gong. The mosses in the gullies, sodden for eleven months of the year, are brittle as tinder and the light breeze that now and again rustles along the heights blows the dead lichen and the rock dust into eyes and hair. The only water less than a long weary trudge away is the tiny spring that has been bubbling out of its shaded rock corner for centuries, and to be aware of this refreshment is a comfort.

Down in the dales the dairy cows stand drowsily in the shade or wade belly deep in the lakes, but on the fells the mountain sheep, still unshorn and heavy with their matted fleeces, stand panting in the blazing sunlight. They look uncomfortable, and the fell farmer will be hoping the wicks don't get at them in the heat. Here and there on the farms they have got in their early hay, but elsewhere there's little growth of grass, although more buttercup than we've had for years.

Reservoir levels are down, waterfalls have dried up and cottage gardens need nightly watering. Horticulturists and water engineers say we need a fortnight's steady rain; innkeepers, boatmen and purveyors of ice cream say we could do with another month of this sort of weather. But it is not the best kind of weather for the high fells, with the distant views obscured by haze, the colours dried up, the clammy heat, the dusty screes and hardly a sight or sound of moving water.

High summer in the hills with the air full of the splashings, cries and murmurings of becks, birds and insects, the new carpet of bracken and here and there the heather, and the luscious bilberry harvest there for the picking can be a joyous time, but it is too early for all this yet. Of late, there have been few splashings and murmurings, although the clegs and the midges have been out, and the succulent blue-black berries of our mountain fruit have yet to appear.

There are, however, compensations for the mountain man on these hot, sticky days, and the best of these are in the tarns, pools and springs. To cleave the waters of Blackmer Pot in Langstrath or Stickle Tarn above Langdale or a score of other places and thrill to the shock of cold water on jaded flesh is to taste real invigoration, and no drink tastes better than ice-cold water from a hidden spring when the perspiration is streaming into your eyes.

Other, slightly more subtle delights, also come to mind – to emerge, for instance, out of a steaming corrie into the fresh air on the ridge or to traverse across oven-hot slabs of rock on a precipice full in the sun into the cool depths of a chimney, guarded perhaps, by wet, glistening walls. On several weekends during the recent heat wave I have been climbing on Dow Crag, where the delights tend to come at the end of the day. Sometimes we have cooled off in the clear

Pavey Ark

depths of Goat's Water before the sun has left the tarn and on other days carried on, above our climb, to the top of the mountain.

Surely there is no more exciting or comprehensive view in Lancashire than from the top of Dow Crag. Six or seven miles away to the northwest, beyond the Hardknott track, the notched line of the Scafells stretches across the sky; southwest through woodlands and past old farmsteads winds Wordsworth's Dunnerdale all the way to the sea; while south, stretched out like a map, is the whole of Furness with Morecambe Bay beyond. It is a view that seems to have everything – sea, sky and mountains, islands, valleys and lakes – and by turning your head you can switch from contemplation of the highest land in England to the sight of sailing craft on Coniston Water far below, ships far out in the Irish Sea, walkers smaller than tin tacks on Brim Fell, the flat dome of Ingleborough and perhaps the glint of a car windscreen somewhere Morecambe way.

This is the ideal ending to a good day on Dow: to emerge out of the darkness of the shadowed crag into the summer sunshine or, on days such as those we have been having recently, to climb out of stuffy heat into a fresh breeze blowing up out of Eskdale and meet the swifts shooting out of the gullies into the evening sky, and then walk quietly down the fellside as the day cools off towards nightfall, with the blue hills for company, the larks still singing and the shadows lengthening across the close-cropped turf …

Most mountain folk will have their favourite pools – perhaps the one below Stanley Gill at Dalegarth, or those of the upper Esk, or others in Longsleddale, or in Wasdale, or in the Derwent among the Borrowdale birches – but my favourite is Blackmer (or Black Moor) Pot in Langstrath. You can undress on the hot rocks and dive in from any height you choose, swim up and down between the canyon-like walls for 40 yards or more, force your way through the waterfall at one end, climb up out of the vertical sides of the pot and bake in the sunshine on the ledges or luxuriate on the turf with the sweet scent of thyme in your nostrils. On a day when the beck slides lazily through the meadows and the sheepdogs, eyes glistening and tongues a-quivering, sprawl panting in the shade, it is well worth the walk to the pool.

Generally, even on the stuffiest day, a breeze steals through the rock gorge and across the water, and dripping mountain plants cling to the vertical walls. You can feel the spray, dancing like a million ice crystals in the sunlight, listen to the roaring of the falls, the splashing and gurgling among the boulders and the tinkling of the sliding pebbles, and peer down into dark, inviting depths that have never known the sun.

The churning waters of a thousand years have carved smooth basins in the solid rock and hewn out the black canyon with its polished, slippery walls. You jump or dive in from your chosen height, and the shock makes you gasp as you go down between the dark walls, but you rise, spluttering, invigorated and a new man, without even touching the bottom.

These are the sorts of places to explore in the Lake District heat wave, and if you pick your dip at the end of the day you can stride home down the valley like a giant refreshed, ready to push over mountains.

SHEEP RESCUE
2 May 1969

The Lakeland year for many active people – and not only the young – is divided at weekends into climbing or fell walking during the summer and skiing in the winter, and the change round often comes almost overnight. One day you put away your skis for the year and inspect your rope and climbing boots, but the personal transition does not always come so easily.

There are still snow patches on the Lakeland hills and I dare say there are places where you could ski at a pinch, but for some of us the season finished a fortnight ago with an energetic day in warm sunshine on one of the last big patches in the district, not far from the Westmorland Harter Fell. This meant that last weekend would be the start of our climbing season, a little late for most people and nearly six months in my case since I had last handled steepish rock. My companion was a friend with whom I had not climbed for many years, and we proposed to celebrate our reunion by repeating a modest first ascent we had made together exactly fifteen years ago.

I could easily remember our discoveries of 1954, but it was much more difficult to recapture anything approaching one's earlier standard. Fifteen years ago these climbs had appeared guileless and straightforward, simple even, but last weekend they were almost desperate ventures on rock that seemed to have steepened by ten or twenty degrees. We had been attracted to Eagle Crag in Grisedale in 1954 because the rock was beautifully rough textured and dried quickly in the sunshine and because we had seen a sheep scrambling safely up the last few feet at the top. Where a sheep could go we could go too, even if we were off-form. And so we made three or four routes, believing we had discovered a new crag, although later we found that one of our climbs had been done earlier, and since then the crag has been developed by very much better climbers than ourselves and is now, I believe, fairly well known.

Nethermost Pike

Since we had originally been attracted to the crag by a sheep, it was odd that the only other climber on the crag last Sunday was another sheep, apparently crag-fast. Sheep normally become crag-fast by working down a rocky fellside in search of the sweeter grasses and herbs, slithering and jumping down walls of rock until eventually they reach a ledge above a vertical drop and find themselves unable to scramble back up the crag. They then apparently resign themselves to their fate, first eating all the grass within reach, until eventually, weakened and exhausted, they fall to their deaths or are rescued.

We could see that this particular sheep had not been there long, for the grass on the ledge, although close-cropped, had not been trodden down as happens when a sheep is trapped for a week or more. The climb, we thought, would have to wait, and we set about the rather complicated business of rescue – complicated because when you are grappling with a Herdwick to tie her up in a cat's cradle of rope all she thinks about is jumping over the edge, carrying her would-be rescuer with her. You, therefore, have to be fairly subtle in a sheep rescue and catch her off her guard.

All this takes time and ingenuity, but we were making satisfactory progress when all at once she tumbled to the situation, took sharp avoiding action, skidded off the ledge, slithered onto a wet, mossy slab, bounced down a couple of short walls, ricocheted into a gully, somer-saulted down a waterfall, crashed onto the screes – and then picked herself up and trotted nimbly away to the nearest patch of grass.

By then it was pouring with rain and the rocks were streaming, but my companion is the sort of person who glories in adversity and discom-fort, and we had to repeat our little climb of 1954, even though our fingers were frozen and the water was running into our boots. Holds that fifteen years ago had seemed ample had shrunk to the tiniest excres-cences, and easy-angled slabs now seemed to soar to the vertical and beyond. How desperate everything seemed after the relaxed ease of skiing, but in eight months' time climbing would, perhaps, have become more natural again and skiing a trial for untrained legs.

Across the ridge lay the magnificent dalehead of Deepdale, one of the most delightful sanctuaries in Lakeland and still surprisingly little known. Here is some of the best rock scenery in the district, many splendid routes and a sense of seclusion almost Highland in its appeal. St Sunday Crag itself is hardly a popular mountain, and yet it dominates the western reach of Ullswater far more dramatically than Helvellyn and commands the whole length of the lake better than any other mountain. The Grisedale face of the fell drops almost 2,000 feet in half a mile, with crags nearly a mile long, and is one of the most dramatic mountain walks in the district. The views of the lake as we came down the long northeast ridge and across the shoulder of Birks made a cloudy, sunless day almost memorable.

Two pairs of ravens were croaking excitedly above us, worried no doubt about their eggs, and far below our feet the lake curved round the side of Place Fell like a shining scimitar, with the tiny islands riding like yachts at anchor. The old Scots pines were reflected in the waters of Lanty's Tarn, the larches on the wooded slopes of Glemara Park were newly sprouting their delicate shade of green, and the smoke from the cottages in Patterdale rose slowly in the evening air.

1970s

Wetherlam

FURY AND MAJESTY
19 June 1970

'No rain to speak of for seven weeks,' said the man from the Water Board the other day, and yet last week I was in the middle of one of the biggest deluges I can recall since monsoon days in Burma twenty-five years ago.

It happened in the Lakeland fells, and after about an hour of it it was easy to understand how some of these places sometimes manage to collect up to 8 inches of rain in a day. The mystery was where all the water went, for an hour later the fells were smiling in the evening sunshine and the ground seemed just as hard and dusty as ever, while down in the valley they were carting water and talking about calling in water diviners.

But before the deluge there were two hours of severe thunder and lightning in the mountains, and the experience of being in among it at its height, although rather alarming at the time, was one I would not have missed. Rarely have I seen mountains in such majestic, angry mood; never have the lightning flashes seemed so close.

It was one of the hottest and stuffiest days of what may be a long, hot summer to remember, and the toil up Wetherlam from Coniston by way of Lad Stones was like scrambling up the side of a giant Turkish bath. The last people I saw on a 12 mile walk over ten tops were some boys bathing in the waterfalls of Church Beck, and I saw nobody else until I returned to the village some hours later. I soon envied the boys splashing about in the cool water for, although I was stripped to the waist, the perspiration was pouring off my head and face in a constant stream, my rucksack seemed glued to my back and the air was so heavy that you felt you were walking through blankets.

As I toiled higher the air became even more oppressive and the heat haze closed in around me until I could hardly see Tilberthwaite. And then, just before reaching my first summit, the thunder, which had been growling in the distance for some time, suddenly exploded a few miles to the north and the first lightning flashes stabbed across the sky. From the top of Wetherlam the Lakeland fells, from the trough of Wrynose Bottom to the Scafells, looked exactly like a scene from Dante's *Inferno*.

The heat haze had been transformed into a boiling, black cauldron of cloud, with dark pillars of mist reaching to the sky and dark grey whirlpools of vapour swirling about the valleys. It looked infinitely menacing, and I was wondering whether anybody was in the middle of it when suddenly the lightning cracked immediately overhead and the thunder seemed to rock the very mountain top.

I continued on to the secondary summit of Black Sails, nearly a mile away, with the lightning flashing and the thunder rolling all around me, but it was not until I was descending into the gap of Swirl Hause, before the ascent of Prison Band to the top of Swirl How, that the fury of the storm really exploded. The lightning jagged down from the heavens, first just ahead of me and then just behind, until I was convinced that Jove was sitting up above with his thunderbolts, trying to get my range. One particularly vicious flash struck the rocks about 50 yards behind me, and a sheep, quietly cropping the turf, suddenly exploded into life and ran helter-skelter across the fellside, baa-ing piteously in obvious alarm. And a raven, sailing past the crags, fled, croaking wildly, to the south.

It was possible to judge, more or less, where the lightning was striking and – on the assumption that lightning only strikes the same place once – I kept hurrying on to try to reach these places in time, although realising, of course, that the chances of being hit were very remote indeed. The thunder was deafening, the air was full of noise and flashes, and each clap of thunder reverberated round the crags like a drum-roll.

And then, on the top of Great Carrs, I saw the mothballs, rolling along the ground ahead of me, as if they had dropped out of my pocket, and a moment later things started dropping on my head and back. They were, of course, hailstones, the size, shape and colour of mothballs, and soon there were thousands of them dropping out of the sky and rolling down the fellside. An hour before I had been sweltering in oppressive heat, but now pieces of ice were falling out of the sky and the air was suddenly chilled.

After the two Carrs I walked up Greyfriar and had my sandwiches by the cairn, and it was not until I was on the way down to Great How Crags that the really heavy rain began. All the way along the ridge line, above the crags and then on to Brimfell, Coniston Old Man, Dow Crag and Buck Pike, the deluge continued, and I was soon wet through to the skin and my boots full of water. The rain really did seem to be coming down in stair-rods, right out of the east, but the ground soaked it up immediately, and the familiar squelching through Lakeland bog in heavy rain was absent. To the east the sky was one black curtain, and I'm sure an inch of rain must have fallen in that hour. Once wet through it was pleasant enough, and the scramble up the wet rocks was a welcome change from the dusty toil of earlier in the day.

I carried on over Brown Pike and down to the Walna Scar track where the sun came out, and I dried myself out near the old, familiar stones of Cove Bridge. The larks were singing as I came down the well-known track to Coniston where the early evening looked as hot and sunny as it had been for weeks.

I remembered, as I came down the track across Little Arrow Moor, a June day just ten years ago when I had walked down the same path from Dow Crag in a thunderstorm that had transformed a dusty, dried-up landscape into a tilted swamp, alive with a hundred rivers, and a hot, sultry summer afternoon had become an inferno of noise and fury. But this had been a sudden storm, blowing up in half an hour, whereas last week the preliminaries had been boiling up for hours and the deluge was even heavier. Yet after the storm there were no new becks rushing down the fellsides, just the same dried-up watercourses and the lakes and tarns as low as ever – Levers Water, for instance, only about half its normal size.

They say we are in for a long, dry summer, but the rain, when it comes, could last for weeks, for three successive dry summers, say the Water Board men, are extremely rare.

Twenty years ago Lakeland had one of its worst Augusts ever when 27 inches of rain fell on the Seathwaite fells – more rain than some parts of the country get in a whole year. However bad the drought, most of us hope this does not happen again.

THE CLEAN AND LONELY HOWGILLS
11 December 1970

The motorist, driving northwards along the new Westmorland motorway, sees, just before he enters the Tebay gorge, a great wall of smoothly sculptured hills towering high up on his right-hand side – his first close-up view of real mountains. These are the Howgill Fells, the nearest hills to any motorway but among the least known hills in the country. Thousands of motorists now drive past them every week, admiring, if they care for these things, their bulky symmetry and the cloud shadows chasing across sunlit slopes, yet you can walk along the whole range and never meet a soul.

For more than a hundred years railway travellers en route to Scotland must have noticed these hills as their trains swung into the gorge, while the motorists in the southern areas of the Lake District National Park can see them along the eastern skyline.

Seen from my house, the Howgills appear to bask all day in whatever sunshine there may be – a long line of gentle switchback summits, suggesting, because of their smooth bulk, sleeping elephants. But not everybody sees them in this way. One beautifully accurate description in an old book portrays them as 'humpbacked hills as sleek as sealskin and reflecting the sunlight like shot silk', but the poet Norman Nicholson thought the range looked like a row of mud pies.

Although the Howgills are as attractive, in their own way, as many other parts of Lakeland, they are outside the Lake District National Park, and most of the range is also outside Westmorland, with the West Riding county boundary winding round the back of the higher fells. Westmorland claims Tebay Fell at the northern end of the range and the Langdale Fells further to the east – a much lonelier mountain country than the well-known Pikes above Dungeon Ghyll. Boundary changes hang on much more practical matters than scenery, but Westmorland would be a much more compact and neatly shaped county if it included all this fine fell country.

Two of us went over the whole length of the range the other day from Tebay to Sedbergh – you need a car at each end – and saw

The Howgill Fells

nobody from the time we left the motorway until we looked down from Winder several hours later at the boys playing rugger in the school fields a thousand feet below. Earlier we had seen the Euston to Glasgow express racing alongside the river and through the gorge – just like watching a child's train from a roof – and now and again we had glimpses of the motorway – a shiny, dark ribbon laid around the contours and then straight as an arrow towards the estuary.

I remembered the last time I had been on the Howgills – on skis before the motorway was started – and decided that the new road had not spoiled the view. From this height it seems a very slight intrusion, completely dwarfed by the surrounding hills, and no more than another feature in the view, like the railway and the river. But, mostly, when you are walking along the spine of the Howgills you are out of sight of both the motorway and the railway and amid a surprisingly complex cluster of hills that soar and dip in all directions.

Seen from the west or even from the motorway, the Howgills look like a long chain of fells, but when you are on top you realise you have been looking at only one side and that the area is a jumble of heights with valleys running all ways and no central ridge line. Indeed, the Howgills are a circle of hills rather than a range. Here is a country of deep ravines and sweeping ridges, of waterfalls and shy becks sliding through tilted moraines – a clean, lonely country with just a few sheep, the ravens and the larks, fresh air all round and long views deep into Yorkshire.

Except at the Sedbergh end, the Howgills are largely untracked, and we had to steer at times by compass through the mist that enveloped the summits but later was swept away by strong winds rushing up the ridges from the southwest. This is the finest sight the mountain walker ever gets in the hills: the sight of mists clearing from the tops and the dale suddenly leaping upwards from below your feet. It seemed strange to have to use a compass in hills I can see from my house, but I have neglected the Howgills just like nearly everybody else.

The names of the fells may sound unfamiliar to mountain folk used to Lakeland – The Calf, Brant Fell, Bram Rigg, Fell Head, Uldale Head, Simon's Seat, Rispa Pike and many more – but they are far from unworthy. True, they are smooth and featureless on the tops, but many of them have remarkably steep ridges sloping down into the valleys, while the ravines, especially Carlin Gill with the fine cleft of Black Force, are a feature not often seen in neighbouring Lakeland. Cautley Spout is the one tourist attraction of these fells – a torrent of water precipitated down the fellside in three fine leaps, in full view from the Kirkby Stephen road and a splendid sight when in spate.

But it is the impression of massive sculpturing that makes the real appeal of these lonely hills, sculpturing you don't often get in the Lakeland fells, except perhaps on Blencathra. They seem to react to the play of sunlight and shadow much more than do less smoothly shaped mountains, and this modelling is especially noticeable under snow. When draped in snow from top to bottom and lit from the side by strong sunlight to expose the great gashes of the shadowed ravines, the Howgills can have something of the appearance of an Alpine range. Potentially, too, this is the finest skiing area in the north of England. The hills are smooth and rounded, with little or no heather, no stone walls, few crags and screes and short fell grass that needs only a slight covering of snow to be negotiable. Unfortunately for the skier, however, the hills, being lower, attract less snow than the Lakeland hills and the northern Pennines, while the best slopes face west and southwest so that the snows have to be quickly seized before they disappear.

We went over eight summits the other day and did not see one scrap of litter and only a very occasional boot-print. This is what the Lake District was like forty years ago.

THE FORGOTTEN PEAKS
5 February 1971

Two of the most neglected mountains in Lakeland, Caudale Moor and Red Screes, also happen to be among the most easily accessible, their summits being only a thousand feet or so above the inn on top of Kirkstone Pass. If hard pressed, you could run up and down Red Screes in an hour, and although Caudale Moor on the other side of the pass is much further away, it is a very simple walk – even in mist – and need not take much longer. And yet, with the advantage of a start at 1,500 feet above sea level, surprisingly few people bother to go onto these fells, and there's not even a track up the rocky front of Red Screes, although the summit is less than half a mile away.

By a coincidence, I happened to be on both these fells on successive weekends, the second time being last Sunday when, having been blown off Cross Fell by the wind, I was returning over Kirkstone Pass and thought the snow in the combe below the summit of Red Screes might be interesting and sheltered from the northerly gale.

The steep snow and the ice on the rocks made the ascent well worth while, but driving snow and thick mist on the summit restricted visibility to a few yards, and the wind, which had rocked my parked car on top of the pass, was even more violent at 2,500 feet. It is this craggy, eastern face of Red Screes that is the mountain's principal glory, for the western slopes into Scandale are uninteresting and the long trudge up the shoulder of the fell from Ambleside is not particularly rewarding. Red Screes looks rather like a steeply breaking wave – smooth on one side and almost beetling on the other – and from my house this craggy wall seems to tower high above the Garburn Pass, although it is 3 or 4 miles further on. As I write, I can just pick out the snow gully where I went up, but the clouds are massing for more snow and the picture will soon be blotted out.

In wintertime, with the dark crags showing like shadows under the white wave, Red Screes looks impregnable, but a good walker can scramble up quite easily, provided he has an ice axe. You can choose between either of the twin combes, threading a way through the crags or following the snow gullies that steepen into a cornice below the summit ridge in a good winter.

In summertime you notice the colour of the crumbling scree slopes that gives the fell its name, but the crags above the scree are too shattered for climbing, and the whole face is a good example of a disintegrating mountain. A boulder that fell out of these rocky combes years ago gave Kirkstone its name, and it still lies at the top of the pass, its shape vaguely suggesting a church tower.

On a good day the view from the summit is quite extensive, with most of Windermere mapped out below you, a glimpse of the Yorkshire hills to the southeast, a long peep into Patterdale and many of the most shapely mountains in Lakeland standing up all round the horizon. From near the summit you feel you could hurl a stone at the inn more than a thousand feet below, and in wintertime, when it is really still, you can almost hear voices down on the pass.

One feature of the summit is the presence of a small tarn and several satellite ponds, not more than 20 yards away – one of the few examples of summit tarns in Lakeland. Presumably they rely on rainwater entirely, but the largest was full last Sunday, although

Red Screes and Kirkstone Pass

neatly sheeted in bearable ice. I am told that this tarn is full of
tadpoles in summer, although I've never noticed any there.

Alfred Wainwright, the guidebook writer, claims for Red Screes
the greatest mileage of stone walls of any fell east of the Keswick to
Windermere road. This may be true, for any mountain is surrounded
by them, but Caudale Moor on the opposite side of the pass is also
girt about with stone walls on all sides, and indeed, there is a wall
running all the 2½ miles from the inn to the summit.

This is why I wrote earlier that Caudale Moor is a very simple
walk, even in mist, although the walls do make it a dull one. But
although there is little challenge in Caudale Moor from the main

road, the mountain is really a complicated mass of considerable character. Craggy ridges run off the summit plateau in several directions, and the mountain's subsidiary summits include Hartsop Dodd, Hart Crag, Pike How and St Raven's Edge. In addition, Caudale Head is a fine, rocky cirque, and Raven Crag, overlooking the lovely valley of Pasture Beck, is one of the steepest crags in the district.

Indeed, if you include all its outliers, Caudale Moor is really one of the most extensive mountains in Lakeland, embracing all the area between Kirkstone Pass, Pasture Beck and the Trout Beck, yet most people driving over Kirkstone don't even know its name, and it is rarely mentioned in the guidebooks. But, especially in wintertime, you can really savour the desolation and loneliness of unspoiled fells on Caudale Moor, a fell where the red deer, the fell ponies and the foxes roam undisturbed. I have watched a fox for nearly half an hour, taking his ease in the snow above Threshthwaite Mouth, seen red deer and fell ponies in Woundale and, at the end of the day, spotted an old buzzard sitting in a tree by Pasture Beck.

The actual summit of Caudale Moor is Stony Cove Pike, and the term John Bell's Banner really applies only to the lower summit of the moor. The Rev. John Bell was a curate of Ambleside, banner is the old word for boundary, and at one time the various parishes met on Caudale Moor, so that the summit became known locally as the limit of Mr Bell's ministrations. This was nearly 400 years ago, before Ambleside became a separate parish.

Seen from the head of the Troutbeck valley, Caudale Moor comes into its own as a splendid, rocky mountain, and to walk round it is a tramp of at least 10 miles. There are ancient settlements, deserted quarries, old mine workings, a cluster of tiny tarns near the summit and many other things to discover.

Long years ago – there are few trees now – they say that a squirrel could have passed from the edge of Windermere to the rocks at Threshthwaite Mouth without touching the ground. But there was no sign of life on Caudale Moor the other weekend, and I don't think I've ever met anybody on the fell or on Red Screes – even when Kirkstone top is crowded with people.

A GIANT SPECTRE
12 February 1971

A gigantic, ghostly figure, perhaps 50 feet high, stood in the mist on the edge of the mountains that look down on Stake Pass. Behind the figure, and throwing it into high relief, were ringed concentric circles of gold, blue and red, as if the heavens were on fire, and for a moment the earth stood still in wonder at the glory of the vision.

But this colossus striding the heavens was no wrath of God nor even a Lakeland version of the Grey Man of Ben Macdhui, but just our old friend the Brocken Spectre. I raised my arm, and the apparition, standing on the ridge a mile away, raised his; I climbed upwards into the mist, and the vision did the same.

In more than forty years' experience of the mountains it was, I think, only the fourth Brocken Spectre I had seen, and the sight, normally coming in unusual weather, is always a memorable experience, and, to match it, this winter has so far been the strangest I can remember. Already it is mid-February and winter has not yet begun. Apart from a couple of falls early in the season there has been no snow to speak of, the high roads of the district have remained open, the buds are sprouting in the gardens, and on a sunny morning the birds are singing as if spring is already here.

For the skier and the mountaineer it has so far been the worst winter we can remember; for the elderly and, perhaps, for the weekend motorist, it has been the best. The primroses are out in my garden, 500 feet above sea level, and rhododendrons have been breaking into colour in the south of Scotland.

There was a sudden blizzard of snow a fortnight ago – with flakes as big as fifty new pence – but the ground was so warm that none of it settled, even for five minutes. And the next day, for a few hours, there were gale-force winds in places, almost the only winds of this quiet, mild winter that has yet to begin. Not only has it been the mildest and most snow-free winter that I can remember, but it has been almost completely free from wind, and I speak from experience here, for my house is particularly exposed and it can be windy here when it is calm everywhere else. But for weeks now the trees have

Langdale Pikes, from Chapel Stile

hardly stirred, and there is an ominous stillness in the air that suggests some cataclysmic upheaval to come. For, by all the laws of averages, the hard winter is still to come, and spring, despite the chirping of the birds, can hardly yet be round the corner.

It was on one of these strange, quiet February days recently that I saw my Brocken Spectre from the upper slopes of Bowfell. In some ways it was one of the most remarkable winter days I had had in the hills in years – a day sandwiched between days of hill fog that have been hanging over the district on and off for weeks. In the head of Langdale the farmers were manuring the fields, and river board men were working in the beck in the sunshine. The smoke rose straight in the air from the farmhouse chimneys. It was warm enough to walk without sweater or anorak, and huge, white, billowy clouds hung motionless about the mountain tops. Patches of snow could be seen peeping through the clouds on Crinkle Crags, while aircraft carved their vapour trails in the blue heavens above the Pikes.

I went into the clouds somewhere above the top of The Band, and it was high up on the rocky east ridge of Bowfell, not far below the summit, that I saw the Brocken Spectre. The white clouds were patchy at this point, and when I was crossing the top of one of the gullies I noticed a movement or a shadow on my right and, stopping, saw the Spectre outlined, through the mist, on a distant ridge.

The sun was shining through the fleecy clouds above Crinkle Crags, which were exactly behind me as I faced across the hidden dale to Langstrath, and my image was photographed onto the thin mist across the valley. It must have been exactly the right combination of cloud and sunshine to produce the effect. One has been in the mountains in sunshine and clouds on hundreds of occasions without seeing the Brocken Spectre.

The circular rainbow behind the huge figure striding the skies was much more spectacular than in the other Brocken Spectres I remember. In effect, there were three different rainbow rings within each other, each one a kaleidoscope of colour.

The apparition disappeared as I went up towards the summit across patches of hard snow, glistening in the sunlight. There was nobody on top – I saw nobody on the hills all day – and the familiar view from the summit was, on this occasion, quite breathtaking. From my perch I looked down rocks and snow patches towards Langdale and Langstrath on the one side and distant Dunnerdale on the other, but the mountains, all round the compass, were hidden behind a sea of fleecy white cloud that filled the upper part of the dales.

But, here and there around the horizon, tiny islands of grass and rock – the highest mountain tops – floated on the white sea just below the bluest of blue skies out of which the sun beat down on the snow as it does in the Alps in spring. Some of the tiny islands were easy to identify – the Scafells, for instance – but I had to take a compass bearing on one island almost due north to confirm that it was, in fact, the summit of Glaramara. But slowly, as I ate my sandwiches at the summit, the white clouds melted away and the mountains came back into the picture.

It would have been warm enough for sunbathing in the snow, for there wasn't enough wind to disturb a match flame, and yet only a few days earlier I had been nearly blown off Cross Fell by an 80 mile an hour gale. And there was ice on the pools of Three Tarns and ice on the rocks, out of the sun, on the way over Crinkle Crags. At the end of the ridge I left the sunlight and went down the shadowed ravines in Oxendale towards the farms at the head of Langdale. Perhaps this is the wrong way round to do this walk on a sunny winter's day, for it means finishing in the shadows, but the pools in the Oxendale ravines make a wonderfully refreshing end to a summer's day, although I decided they were far too cold on this occasion.

There was every reason to be well satisfied with this simple day, for the following day, and for several days afterwards, Lakeland was cloaked in damp mist with little or nothing to be seen – and certainly not the glories of sunlight and snow, blue skies and white clouds and the Brocken Spectre.

A MAGICAL PLACE OF MEMORIES
26 March 1971

There are many Mosedales in the Lake District, dotted about the map from Crummock in the west to Mungrisdale in the east with several in between, but probably the best known is the one beneath a glorious cirque of mountains, tucked round the corner of Wasdale Head. This is the one they had in mind in this week's television play, *The Mosedale Horseshoe*, for the traverse of the fells around the dale makes one of the best ridge walks in the district, although perhaps not so popular as the Fairfield Horseshoe, which is now regularly run round each summer – up and down all eight tops – in less than an hour and a half. But the Mosedale Horseshoe, done properly, is worth savouring so as to fill in most of the day.

None of the Lakeland Mosedales have anything to do with Moses, although the legendary Moses Rigg, smuggler and path-maker, gave his name to several features around Wasdale. The name simply derives from moss, which is the Lakeland name for a bog, and, if you think about it, all the Mosedales have boggy sections, the Wasdale one having its bog high up and the head of the dale with starry saxifrage sprouting through the wet moss in places.

The Eskdale Mosedale – often spelled Moasdale – is always wet below the ridge that looks down to the Lingcove Beck, while the little-known Mosedale that wanders towards Wet Sleddale or Swindale from the Gatescarth track is as boggy a place as you can find in these parts. But the bog by no means ruins these lonely places. I have the greatest affection for the Moasdale that takes you direct from Hardknott to the highest land in England through some of the wildest country in Lakeland.

The Wasdale Mosedale, surrounded by its rocky ring of fells, is for me a magical place with many memories of youthful adventure more than forty years ago. I remember, for instance, returning to a camp site by Ritson Force, so sunburned by the scorching heat on the Napes Ridges where I had been climbing that sleep was out of the question, so we went on a midnight walk. And I remember climbs on Elliptical Crag, high up the dale and just below Wind Gap, always a wet place, for the fellside drains down the face of the crag so that on a hot day you could generally keep cool. Further down the valley there is the Y-Boulder – easily recognised by its Y-shaped crack. There are nearly a score of climbing routes on this lump of rock, many of them quite hard, and I must have fallen off most of them from time to time. One of them, demanding a fair amount of agility, can be done feet first!

I think my most amusing Mosedale memory is that of a walk up the dale to climb on Pillar Rock nearly forty years ago. There were three of us, and I think it was one of the most miserable days for weather I have ever endured in the fells, although enlivened by some exhilarating talk from my companions, who happened to be pioneer mountaineers of some distinction. The rain sheeted down steadily all day, whipped into a whirling maelstrom as we neared the top of Black Sail Pass, and visibility was restricted to about 2 yards. There were no rain and windproof anoraks and cagoules in those days, just tweed jackets, and we were soaked to the skin. We stopped at the head of the pass to get our bearings and wipe the rain out of our eyes and wondered whether anybody else could possibly be out in the fells on such a day, let alone on the way to do some rock climbing.

And then, suddenly, out of the gloom and almost at our elbow, we heard a voice. 'Excuse me, can you tell me the way to Whitehaven?' and a strange figure stepped into our midst. He was wearing, quite sensibly, a sou'wester and a yellow oilskin cape and – almost unbelievably – was carrying a bicycle on his back. We understood that he had scrambled up the pass from Ennerdale – 1,800 feet of it, carrying his bike – and had now lost his way.

When we had recovered from our astonishment, we directed him down the fell towards Wasdale, 2 or 3 miles away, and explained his route from there to Whitehaven, and in a moment he was swallowed up again in the mist, bike and all. We certainly admired his determination and later wondered which of us was more stupid and single-minded. I hope he got his bicycle down to

The Mosedale Horseshoe

Wasdale, a 4 mile carry from Ennerdale. For our part, we went up the North Climb on Pillar and down Central Jordan, finishing up at the end of the day like three drowned rats, but quietly glad we'd been out.

But the great joy of Mosedale is the traverse of the ring of fells that encircle the dale. Ideally, this should start with the ascent of Yewbarrow and finish with the traverse of Kirk Fell, but most people miss these out and content themselves with Red Pike, Scoat Fell, Steeple and Pillar, dropping down to Black Sail and then back to Wasdale through Mosedale. Even so, it is a splendid walk, especially along the ridge of Red Pike, with its long line of cliffs dropping down to the Mosedale Beck, and the fine high-level walk along the Pillar fells. The wild coves under Steeple are particularly impressive, and this is among the most rugged country in Lakeland.

Most walks around the Mosedale Horseshoe start and finish at Ritson's Force, the little waterfall perhaps half a mile up the dale from the hotel. This was named in 1895 by M.J. Baddeley, a guidebook writer who died at Bowness sixty-five years ago. Mr Baddeley wrote, rather pontifically, in one of his *Thorough Guides* to the Lake District: 'We have ourselves taken the liberty of naming the charming little force above the inn after our hero.'

His hero was, of course, the famous Auld Will Ritson, the redoubtable dalesman who kept the Wasdale inn last century and became a legend in his lifetime, and the name has now crept onto the larger scale maps. Many years ago I was chatting to a relative of Auld Will, the late Mr John Ritson Whiting, who kept the hotel for many years before the last war. He was leaning on a wall beyond Ritson Force – his 'garden fence' he called it – and looking up Mosedale, as he did every day of his life. 'The finest little valley in England,' he told me, and he could have been right.

We certainly thought so as youngsters when we ran down the Dore Head screes after a long day on the tops or the crags, but now the screes have all been scratched away and television has penetrated into the sanctuary.

WALKING INTO NEW PLEASURES
19 May 1972

When the walker has been up all the principal mountains of the Lake District by all the well-worn routes there is still plenty of unfamiliar country for him to explore. He can seek out the lesser known summits he has missed, follow the mountain becks and streams to their sources, visit all the tarns and pools – collecting perhaps a dozen in a day – or invent new ways up and down the fells. After all, the tracked routes to the mountain tops are just the easiest or most straightforward ways – not necessarily the most interesting – and it is surprising how a route just the other side of a familiar ridge or round the corner of a crag can take you into completely new country.

Although I have been walking and climbing in the Lakeland fells for something like half a century, I can generally find something new. This is because I try to avoid tracks whenever possible and aim to familiarise myself with all sides of all the fells, not just the better known routes up and down. For many reasons I prefer to walk alone in the hills in summer or in settled weather but have companions when climbing or on winter expeditions. This is not a recommended procedure for the inexperienced, but it suits me very well.

The other day I was on the Scafell range, having reached the top by a route up Seathwaite Fell, the flank of Great End and the soft snow of Cust's Gully, which was still at least 3 feet deep. Later in the day, having wandered across most of the highest land in England, I was making my way down the untracked slopes of Broad Crag when I thought I would have a look at two places I had not visited for years.

Thousands of people go up to Scafell Pike every year – sometimes hundreds in a single day – but not one in a hundred of them ever go on to the top of Broad Crag, one of the seven 3,000 foot summits of the Lake District and no more than a hundred yards or so from the main highway. It is this neglect of worthwhile places – Lingmell, only a quarter of a mile away from the Corridor Route, is another example – that prompted this article. This and the fact that when I happened to tell two mountain friends where I had been neither had even heard of the places. Although both have been climbing and walking in Lakeland for years, neither had been to either Round How or Lambfoot Dub nor had any idea where they are. Perhaps this is because there are no tracks to either place, which, for me, is an added commendation, and yet the well-marked Corridor Route passes along the foot of the crags of Round How, while the delightful tarn of Lambfoot Dub lies only a couple of hundred feet higher than the same track.

Round How is a little fell of about 2,300 feet – about the height of Pike o' Blisco – which lies on the northern slopes of Broad Crag, above the Corridor Route and above and between the ravines of Greta Gill and Piers Gill. It is partly encircled by crags but connected by easy, sloping fellsides to an amphitheatre that lies below the northern cliffs of the Scafell Pike massif. Several small tarns lie in this amphitheatre, but, as there are no signs of any tracks in the area, I can only assume that hardly anybody ever goes there. I gained the summit of Round How by an easy scramble up the rocks, although an easy walking route could have been found.

Scafell Pike, from Lingmell

From the top you can see people, like tiny matchsticks, passing along the roof-tree of England on their way to the Pike and then turn round and look at the whole southern front of Great Gable with Wasdale lying between. Apart from the distant matchsticks on Broad Crag, I seemed alone in the world for you are too far above the Corridor Route to hear the traffic down there. But then I saw a tiny figure running down the steep slopes of Great End, and he carried on running, all without spotting me, and then across the rocky fellside to the Lingmell col. He was obviously a fell-runner, stripped for the part and perhaps practising for a race, and, like me, was avoiding the tracks but using his feel for the land to work his way across rough country in the most interesting and least demanding way. I greatly admired his fitness for he ran all the way, uphill, to the Lingmell col.

You can see Lambfoot Dub from the top of Round How and also from the slopes of Broad Crag, and its gentle curving shape makes the reason for the name quite plain. It is one of the loveliest of the small tarns of Lakeland, set on a rocky ledge in magnificent wild scenery. From the tarn you look across the great trough of Wasdale to the crags and gullies of Great Gable, and there are peeps down Borrowdale and, at your back, the ridgeline of the Scafells. A perfect place in evening sunlight, with only the larks for company.

I make you a present of these two places off the beaten track, but there are hundreds more that you can find for yourselves. And finding them can be one of the joys of walking the Lakeland hills, especially to those who think they know the fells fairly well. Many of them are not identified on the 1 inch Ordnance Survey map – Round How is shown but not Lambfoot Dub – but the 2½ inch may be found more helpful.

There is talk in Scotland of temporarily closing certain hill tracks so that they can be given the opportunity to recover from the pressure of human feet, and there are even more eroded places in the Lake District. But the walker who prefers to find his own way about the fells rather than following the way everybody else has gone for a hundred years or more is avoiding kicking the hills to death and finding new places he may not have known existed.

THE DODDS AND DEEPDALE
14 June 1974

Deepdale, to many people, is a place where people play football, but to others it is the name of several long and rather remote valleys in the Lake District.

I have often written about the best of the Deepdales – the lonely valley that leads up to the Fairfield crags – but never, I think, about the one that lies 5 miles away to the northwest, at the back of the Dodds. It is an untracked, boggy place, having little to commend it except solitude, and very few people go there, but the circumnavigation of the dale by walking over the surrounding heights can have its quiet rewards on the right sort of day, for the range of the Dodds is not only perhaps the least known bit of Lakeland but also one of the best promenades from which to view the northern fells and dales.

I have never met anybody on the Dodds – except when we've been skiing on Stybarrow Dodd – and the litter wardens could walk the whole range and never find a piece of orange peel or even a beer can ring. Last weekend there were crowds of tourists at Aira Force – the police were there early in the morning putting out their No Parking cones on the roadsides when we passed – but there was nobody in Deepdale where Aira Beck begins with a long cascade of smaller waterfalls and many superb pools.

Dowthwaitehead, at the entrance to the dale, stands at more than 1,300 feet above sea level and in wintertime is one of the loneliest places in the Lake District. For months it rarely sees the sun, and the snows often linger here until late spring. The little cluster of old buildings has an air of dereliction, and I think only two families live there now. There are said to be many more buzzards living at Dowthwaitehead than people, and it was not far from here, some years ago, that I once had a curious encounter with a brown owl that sat on an old stone wall and looked at me, unblinking, for several minutes, as if he had never seen a human being before.

I have suggested that this Deepdale is not well known to Lake District visitors, and the name was not even known by one of its residents from whom we asked permission to park a car! But she had at least heard of Great Dodd, the seventeenth highest mountain in the Lake District, which was the first top in our little round of the dale: Great Dodd, Watson's Dodd, Stybarrow Dodd, Green Side, Hart Side and Birkett Fell, renamed from Nameless Fell in honour of the late Lord Birkett. It is a pedestrian sort of round, with no excitements, but with superb views of the Keswick plain, the lakes, the ridges of Blencathra, the last bit of snow on the Helvellyn cornices and the lonely trough of Deepdale far below.

The larks were singing as we trod the springy upland turf, and the dale was alive with the sound of rushing waters after the recent heavy rains. There was a hail storm on the top of Watson's with a few flakes of snow, but on Stybarrow the ground was steaming in the sunlight, and you felt you could throw a stone onto Raise a mile away.

On the map the Dodds look curiously bare of feature and even of printing, with fewer crags, woods, tarns or other incident than anywhere else in Lakeland (except, possibly, the 'back o' Skiddaw'),

Clough Head and Great Dodd

and this is an accurate representation. There are, indeed, no crags, except some down by the Thirlmere road, no tarns to speak of (just a couple of pools), almost no sculpturing of the mountainsides, little heather and bracken – just five miles of grass.

But the north- and east-facing slopes of these smoothly shaped fells are among the steepest in the Lake District, and the area is potentially the best I know for advanced skiing.

For most people, however, the charm of the Dodds will be the loneliness, the quietude, the splendid, springy turf and the feeling that you can look out, all round the compass, at more spectacular mountains from a high terrace devoid of cairns, litter or much evidence of the passage of feet. This is what Great Gable and the Scafells were like fifty years ago. And in wintertime a lone tour of the Dodds, on skis or on foot, can be more rewarding than a walk up other mountains when everybody else seems to be doing the same thing.

There is an old coach road that contours the skirts of these northern hills, taking you from Dockray to Threlkeld, and I remember once starting from this road and doing a similar round in midsummer and not seeing a soul all day. It was a day when the Lakeland fells looked as sharp against the blue sky as if they'd been cut out of cardboard, when the smoke rose straight from the chimneypots in the valley and when you could almost hear the insects talking.

The Dodds are so featureless that you come upon the little rocks of Calfhow Pike or the boulders of Randersike with some relief, but if you are there on the right sort of day the loneliest fells in Lakeland need not be dreary.

It is strange how little we know about the Dodds – the Ordnance Survey prefers Dod, but Dodds seems to have become accepted. Why, for instance, are they called Dodds? Who was Watson of Watson's Dodd? Why was Nameless Fell so called before Lord Birkett helped to prevent Ullswater from becoming a reservoir? What is the strange ditch across the summit of Hart Side? What is the story behind Fishers Wife's Rake on Clough Head? And who was Jim of Jim's Fold?

There are, as I have said, no crags worth mentioning on the fells, but low down on Watson's, near the roadside, there is the wonderfully steep Castle Rock of Triermain – a romantic-sounding name – and below Clough Head, Wanthwaite Crags and Bram Crag. And there are several splendid ravines, including Stanah Gill and Mill Gill with their waterfalls, and quite a lot of rough country besides, but all crowded down on the western sides, just above the road – a most unusual feature for Lakeland. These western becks are diverted into Thirlmere to supply thirsty Manchester, and the cascades of Aira Beck on the other side of the Dodds are tapped to supply part of rural Cumbria, but the waterworks are hardly noticed in this expansive scenery.

Deepdale itself is best traversed in wintertime when the bogs are frozen or covered in snow. In summer it is better to keep to the heights and at least keep your feet dry. And as you go round the skyline, stop awhile on some of the summits and ponder whether the Ordnance Survey people have even been up there. For the summit cairns seem to be in the wrong places – both on Great Dodd and Stybarrow Dodd – and not on the highest points.

You have to look for little things like this on the Dodds where there's nothing but grass and sky, but if you feel rather lazy or want to be alone or would like to see the Lake District from a new angle these lonely fells might well be the answer on a bright June morning.

WHEN TO HANG UP
YOUR BOOTS
6 June 1975

The recent dry weather has encouraged a return to the crags, and I have been wondering at what age climbers should retire from their sport. Ski racers seem to retire in their twenties, most rugger players in their thirties, and perhaps racing motorists in their forties, but mountaineers seem to be different. Some climbers, of course, regard themselves as too old at forty or fifty and, thereafter, cease to climb, while others, with a lifetime of mountaineering activity behind them, carry on until their sixties. Two friends of mine, both keen mountaineers, stopped on their sixtieth and sixty-fifth birthdays, respectively. They had each thought out the matter carefully and considered the risks, in view of their declining powers, too great.

By climbing, of course, I mean rock climbing on the crags or winter mountaineering. Walking up Scafell Pike or Great Gable is not climbing but fell walking, a worthy pursuit that is often enjoyed by people in their seventies or eighties. I know people approaching ninety years of age who can still enjoy a day in the hills.

Climbing, however, is an activity that requires technical ability and considerable physical reserves. Mere strength is not nearly so important as the average non-climber imagines, but a considerable sense of balance and a certain amount of agility are certainly necessary. Even more important is the psychological factor, for a climber has to feel at home on small holds in exposed situations – a feeling that is not achieved overnight or in a few days and one that, unless conserved by constant practice, quickly disappears. And herein, I believe, lies the main difficulty for the elderly climber.

Unless he keeps at the game fairly regularly he may find himself after a longish absence from the crags unable to climb fairly easy routes, not because of lack of strength or agility or even technical ability but because of the relatively frightening situation on steepish rock, with a long way to fall. Climbers who wish to continue climbing into their sixties and beyond, therefore, should keep in fairly regular practice, even if only on fairly easy routes. An annual week's climbing holiday in the Lakes is not nearly good enough if there is no practice in between.

For something like thirty years I used to climb almost every weekend, but in recent years my attendances at the crags have not been nearly so constant. As a result, after absences of months, I have found myself not so much out of practice as out of tune with the whole situation. Crags suddenly looked much steeper than I remembered and holds much smaller and further apart. Moves that in the past had been made with ease now seemed enormously difficult, not because of a lack of ordinary climbing ability but simply because, through neglect, I was finding steepish rock intimidating, and therefore, being a little scared, I was climbing badly.

From the Outlying Fells of Lakeland
dedicated to the oldtimers on the fells.

I find that after a long absence from the crags I require three fairly frequent visits to regain reasonable form, not, of course, the form of forty years ago – that has gone for good – but sufficient form to be confident and to enjoy myself.

On the other hand, a friend of mine who is approaching seventy years of age still climbs to a remarkably high standard, with a young 'tiger', half his age, as leader. Our attitudes to the crags differ slightly. I prefer not to climb routes unless I can lead them, whereas he will tackle almost anything, provided he has an able leader. As a result, he is still climbing the routes he was doing forty years ago, whereas my ambitions are nowadays much more modest. But we both still enjoy our climbing, in a rather different way, and when we climb together – on the easier routes – we lead alternate pitches, which is the most pleasant way to climb.

I feel, therefore, that the climber's decision about when to retire from the rocks must vary with the individual. Provided the elderly climber has a long experience of the crags and can continue to climb fairly frequently there seems no reason, if he remains fit and active, why he cannot keep up his climbing into his sixties and seventies. Obviously, he will have to lower his standards, probably very considerably, but he should still be able to get a great deal of enjoyment from his chosen sport.

The elderly climber – if I am an example – is not interested in the desperate routes now being put up by young experts but prefers the old classic climbs or routes with a 'mountaineering' flavour that perhaps bring him to somewhere near the top of the mountain. As an increasingly decrepit climber, I find there are not enough long routes in the lower grades – climbs of varied character that are not too demanding. Sometimes we have to seek out our own, and I found a modest one the other day, the buttress between the two gullies on Great Carrs, which was a pleasant exercise.

Of course, we old stagers do not easily take to all the new equipment and ironmongery. We had to get up the climbs without them and in nailed boots forty years ago. Almost shyly, I've acquired a few nuts and bits of wire, but fortunately, I don't need pitons and étriers for my sort of climbing, which mustn't be difficult enough to be frightening.

THE DESCENT TO HELL
27 June 1975

The recent dry weather in Lakeland has been ideal for the fascinating pursuit of gill scrambling or climbing, a minority sport that merits more adherents. With less water coming down the gills the steeper places are more readily negotiable and the chances of a ducking somewhat lessened. In almost every case the scenery in these deeply cut ravines is impressively wild, and to go up a Lakeland mountain by following the bed of a convenient ravine can generally be curiously rewarding, although, of course, much more difficult than the conventional routes.

Climbing experience is usually required and, indeed, it is possible that there are still one or two Lakeland gills that have not yet been ascended throughout. In most of the others you are unlikely to find much evidence of previous exploration, for gill climbing, like pot-holing, where you can get very wet and even very frightened, is not everybody's game.

Note that I write 'gill' and not 'ghyll'. Gill is a good Old Norse word, but ghyll, which looks Welsh, seems to me little more than a romantic Victorian or Wordsworthian affectation. Baddeley, writing his Lake District guides last century, got it right, referring to all gills in the area as gills – Dungeon Gill, Tilberthwaite Gill and so on – but also giving the Old Dungeon Ghyll Hotel, for this is presumably the correct registered name of the hotel, no matter how misguided about nomenclature the original owners might have been.

But many later authors, and some of the mapmakers, still use the word 'ghyll' in some of the proper names of Lake District names – White Ghyll, for instance, or Taylor Ghyll Force and so on, which I do not think is correct. In his book *Cumberland and Westmorland*, published in 1949, Norman Nicholson, usually very accurate, even had a sub-chapter entitled 'Ghylls', but I notice that in his *Portrait of the Lakes*, published in 1963, which uses the same sub-chapter, he altered the spelling to 'Gills' and retains this spelling throughout the book. Obviously he had seen the light.

Lingmell and Piers Gill

Langdale has some of the finest gills in the Lake District. Dungeon Gill and Mill Gill (or Stickle Gill) are well known, but far better is the splendid cluster of ravines in the branch valley of Oxendale – Hell Gill, Crinkle Gill, Browny (or Brown) Gill and Isaac Gill.

The other day two of us failed to get down the big pitch of Hell Gill, being forced, by streaming, vertical rock and the yawning pools beneath, to escape out of the ravine by one of the walls. Better climbers might have done it, but it is possible that Hell Gill is one of the Lakeland ravines that has still not been climbed keeping in the bed all the way.

Years ago I did Crinkle Gill and Browny Gill, finding them most rewarding. I have also descended Tilberthwaite Gill in spate, but this was a youthful expedition that involved getting wet through to the skin and a certain dare-devilry that does not become me today.

One of the most rewarding descents of a Lakeland gill occurred in the summer of 1921 when a party of climbers, making the first descent of Piers Gill, the great ravine that separates Great End from Lingmell, came upon a man sitting near a waterfall. The man had fallen twice, damaging both ankles, and remarkably had lain in that wild, remote place, subsisting on one sandwich, a small piece of ginger cake and a trickle of water for twenty days. He was a London visitor, a Mr Crump, and when walking from Coniston to Wasdale Head had lost his way in the mist and finally got himself into the wild recesses of Piers Gill, where, in trying to get down, he had sustained his injuries. Widespread searches of the Lakeland fells proved unsuccessful. Nobody, of course, had any idea that he might be in that area and, by that time, all hope of finding him alive had been abandoned.

At that time Piers Gill had only been climbed twice, and the climbers, who possibly did not even know that a man was missing in the fells, were attempting the first descent because the summer was one of the driest and warmest the Lake District has ever known. They thought that with the volume of water that cascades down the pitches vastly reduced they might be able to climb down, and this, in fact, they did.

Imagine, therefore, their shock and surprise at finding Mr Crump sitting, barely conscious, below the Bridge Rock and gazing down the gill. The climbers were able to rope the injured man down the pitches and then take him down the fellside on a stretcher to Wasdale Head. Fortunately, he recovered and, years later, was able to come back to Wasdale and look up at the scene of his terrible experience. He told his rescuers how he had lived in that lonely place for twenty days and nights. Until his strength gave out he had shouted for help and had then tried to compose himself for what must have seemed his approaching end. But for the remarkably warm, dry weather he could not possibly have survived his ordeal, and the fact that he was discovered on the very first descent of the ravine must remain one of the miracles of Lakeland mountaineering.

Not all gills in the fell country are as dramatic or difficult as Piers Gill, but most of them are wonderfully attractive places with pools, waterfalls, often vertical or overhanging walls garlanded with trees, shrubs and ferns, as well as caves, rock arches, water-slides, a tumbled chaos of great boulders and sections of crag. To thread your way up or down all this varied terrain gives plenty of exercise and, usually, a few thrills, with new scenery round every corner and new problems that sometimes only yield to acrobatics performed above deep pools.

Sometimes you may get a ducking or you may have to retreat or escape out of the ravine, but this sort of exploration, with the result often in doubt until the end, is generally good fun and not dangerous to the experienced. The more difficult gills should be avoided by scramblers and walkers, but there are still interesting places in off-the-beaten-track Lakeland for even fairly inexperienced adventurers.

Our failed descent of Hell Gill followed a return, after some years, to Bowfell Buttress. Here we found that the huge flake on the fifth pitch of the Plaque Route had come away from the crag and is now lying in pieces – many tons of it – on the screes.

NAMES THAT TRIP
OFF THE TONGUE
12 September 1975

You could see most of the mountains of the Lake District from the summit of Robinson the other day, except, oddly enough, for Scafell Pike, the highest of them all, which was hidden by the hump of Great Gable. A fine, bulky mountain Robinson, splendidly lording it over the Buttermere plain, the sweep of the road over Newlands Hause and the lovely, unfrequented valley of Little Dale. But what a curious name for a Lake District mountain – it is more like the name of a department store or a garage.

Not so strange, though, when you realise that Robinson is one of the commonest surnames in Cumbria. There are six and a half columns of Robinsons in the Cumbria and North Lancashire telephone directory, nearly 700 entries, which is not far behind the Wilsons with eight columns. Wilson is now probably the commonest surname in Cumbria, closely followed by Robinson, which held the distinction up to ten years ago.

So, if you are going to call a mountain after a person – a practice in common use in the Canadian and American Rockies, and occasionally employed in the Himalayas, as in Everest – Robinson would seem to be fairly appropriate and far better than, say, Smith, Jones or Ramsbottom.

And Robinson the mountain was, in fact, called after a person, although he's been dead now for something like 400 years. The mountain was part of the land bought at the dissolution of the monasteries in Henry VIII's reign by one Richard Robinson: 'All the land called Birknesfeld or Gatescath with the appurtenances lying and being in Buttermere.' Up to that time the mountain had no name, but it was thereafter called Robinson's Fell, later to be shortened to Robinson. The purchaser's son eventually sold the property to one of the Stanleys, but the homely name Robinson has continued ever since.

I like the sound of Robinson for a Lake District mountain name far better than some of the others, like Low Pike, Knott, Middle Dodd perhaps, or Sheffield Pike, which has always seemed to me slightly inappropriate.

It was perhaps appropriate that John Wilson Robinson, one of the pioneers of the Lakeland crags, lived not far from the foot of Robinson for most of his life. Robinson's Cairn near Pillar Rock – recently demolished by vandals for the third year in succession – was his memorial.

Some Lakeland mountains, like Blencathra or Glaramara, have splendidly sounding names that trip well off the tongue, while others, such as Grey Friar, Brandreth, Hindscarth or Stybarrow Dodd, have lovely names redolent of the atmosphere of the fell country. Helvellyn, Great Gable, Crinkle Crags, Swirl How, Red Screes and Pavey Ark also have well-chosen names, but Base Brown is not so pleasing, and Yoke is rather odd.

Two of the best mountain names in Lakeland are those of Pillar and Steeple, which are quite accurate descriptions, but Raise, where we go skiing in winter, is a strange name, sometimes confused with the road pass of Dunmail Raise, while, to add to the confusion, there are also two mountains called High Raise, one near the Langdale Pikes and the other on High Street.

The derivation of some of our mountain names is often obscure. Some may be traced back to Old Norse, while others seem to have

Robinson

Celtic connotations. There has been much argument, for instance, about the derivation of Coniston Old Man, the highest mountain in Lancashire until reorganisation, and even more about the spelling (and the pronunciation) of Dow Crag. It seems likely, however, that the suggested Welsh derivation of the Old Man is far too clever and that the name has something to do with one of the local meanings of 'man', a heap of stones. And although Dow Crag has always been pronounced 'Doe' Crag by climbers, it should not be spelled that way, despite the fact that the adjoining mountain happens to be called Buck Pike. Oddly enough, the local quarrymen generally pronounce Dow Crag as it is spelled, giving it a fine, harsh sound more in keeping with the character of the crag.

Watson's Dodd, north of the Helvellyn range, is another curious name for a mountain, for I have never been able to find out who Watson was, although he was probably some local landowner of centuries ago. John Bell's Banner, however, is rather easier, for John Bell was a curate of Ambleside, and the fell marked the extent of the boundary or banner of his parochial influence.

The derivation of Grasmoor has nothing to do with grass, although it is a particularly grassy mountain and possibly contains more varieties of plant life than any other fell. Grasmoor takes its name from 'gris', the wild boar or young pig, a familiar derivation in Lakeland. Ill Bell is shaped like a bell, but Ill comes from the word meaning evil. I have seen the mountain called Hill Bell on some old maps, but this is probably inaccurate.

The surveyors working on the earlier Lakeland maps probably made many mistakes by misunderstanding the speech of the locals. They would ask the name of a particular mountain, say, and then try to write down what they thought the farmer had said. For example, the shoulder of the Wetherlam ridge, which appears on the map as Lad Stones, has always been known locally as 'La'al Gladstone', while Little Narrowcove on Scafell Pike should really be Little Arrowcove or 'La'al Arra'', as the locals say.

For me one of the most splendidly evocative mountain names in Lakeland is Dollywagon Pike, which seems to convey a picture of happy yokels on a summer holiday, although I'm sure this is not the derivation.

Scafell Pike, the highest mountain in England, was originally the Pikes near Scafell, the Pikes referring to Pikes Crag. Scafell should not be spelt with a 'w' and, of course, should be pronounced with the accent on the first syllable, as in almost all Lakeland names. The local pronunciation is something like 'Scawff'l'. There is also a Great Sca Fell, but this is only a shadow of Scafell itself, being more than 1,000 feet lower.

Just over a mile to the west of Great Sca Fell, in the remote country to the north of Skiddaw, is the gloriously named Great Cockup, a mountain rising to less than 1,700 feet, between Frozen Fell and Little Cockup. I can't however believe that the word has any connection with its modern slang meaning, particularly since there is an especially lovely name given to a feature on the shoulder of the fell, the little pass of Trusmadoor, which is as pleasant-sounding a name as any in the Cumbrian fells.

THE FINAL ARTICLE
19 December 1975

This is the last occasion on which these 'Leaves from a Lakeland Notebook' will appear in this paper. Scribblings of this sort can't go on forever and indeed should never go on too long. Readers, as well as writers, probably know when to stop. Over the years readers have been most generous in their letters and may perhaps be interested if, in this final article, I look back to when the feature began and on some of the changes that have taken place in Lakeland in the meantime.

I started writing this weekly feature in the early summer of 1946 on my return from army service abroad and have continued it, without a break (except for holidays) ever since. This means I must have written something like 1,500 pieces or well over one and a half million words on almost every conceivable Lake District subject, from stone walls to golden eagles and from Herdwick sheep to by-passes and motorways. I see I've even written about public conveniences, the decline in the quality of the beer, the speech of the locals and how to cope with the mowdies, or moles, to the city dweller. Everything seemed of some importance, no matter how slight, at the time, and I hope that the articles might occasionally have brought a breath of fresh air to those marooned in towns.

I can't say I've never repeated myself – some topics have been examined on several occasions – but I hope the approach has always been new and even topical. Occasionally, I've written about Scotland, the Alps or even the Canadian Rockies, and sometimes I've peeped over the border into Yorkshire, but mostly I've dealt with the Lake District, where I have had the good fortune to live and which has been the lodestone of my life. No other place in the world that I have seen has the same magical quality of so much variety in such tiny compass.

When I began writing my 'Lakeland Notebook' nearly thirty years ago I used the rather unimaginative and inaccurate pseudonym of 'Dalesman', but after a few months the then editor of the paper decided that I should be raised out of obscurity and identified. This was the first time that any staff writer's name had appeared in the paper; even sports writers hid their lights under bushels, a big change from the situation today. Once I had been identified, however, I had to answer for my effusions and, during the years, have received hundreds of letters from readers. 'A.H. Griffin, Writer, Kendal' has been fairly common and apparently no trouble to post office sorters. 'A.H. Griffin, Writer, Westmorland' was perhaps more difficult, but they found me all right.

Mostly, the letters have been complimentary, but now and again I have been taken to task. Most difficult have been letters from readers who imagined me to be an authority on birds, flowers, geology and many other subjects and have written asking for expert advice. Unfortunately, however, although my knowledge of the mountains might be fairly extensive, I am very far from being anything approaching an expert in anything else.

The greatest thing that has happened to the Lake District during the past thirty years was its creation as a National Park, and the most serious impact has, of course, been the motor car – much more serious than all the reservoirs, the afforestation, the expanding quarries and all the other recurring problems. The trees have altered the scenery more than anything else during the last half century, but the motor car has changed the very quality of life in the district to a far greater extent than any other factor, and not always for the better.

The problems besetting the Lake District were by no means solved when the area became a National Park, but it was the best possible first step. Without planning to this level the most beautiful part of England could well have been spoiled forever by now. But if most of the recommendations of the Sandford Committee on National Parks receive government approval the Lake District should be able to look forward to a much more secure future. Many things are urgently needed at the highest possible level: agreement that the preservation of the amenities must over-ride the provision of recreational activities, a planned hierarchy of roads, the proper control of mineral exploitation and so on. For years now the motor car has seemed to have priority over everything else – new roads, 'improved' roads, car parks and all the other ancillaries for the motorist – and yet the National Park was not primarily created for the motorist but for the walker. The blatant encouragement of tourism is surely questionable, and I welcome the enterprise of South Lakeland Council in calling upon the County Council to carry out a detailed study into the costs and benefits of tourism – the costs of new roads and car parks set against the commercial benefits.

I see dangers in the deterioration of the quality of life in Lakeland, with increased commercialisation and trivialisation. Look at what has happened to Hawkshead, once an unspoiled, quaint village but now a huge car park surrounded by cafés and knick-knack shops. Too many people, it seems to me, are seeking the crock of gold they believe is lying at the foot of a Lakeland rainbow. Too many people are trying to take something out of Lakeland in the shape of hard cash, and too few people are trying to see what they can put into the district.

Lakeland is of vital importance to the rest of England because of its intrinsic and indigenous values: its fells and dales, lakes and becks, its old stone walls, its peace and quietude. It doesn't need anything to gild the lily unless it is an active encouragement of sheep farming.

For if sheep farming goes – and there is a danger of this – much of the manmade quality of the area will disappear, and scrubland will take over.

Much remains to be done to preserve our heritage in the face of new threats and pressures. I'm sure the Lake District, as we love it, will last out my lifetime. My hope is that it will also last out the lifetime of generations to come, but this is unlikely to happen without a great deal of self-sacrifice and dedication.

THE HIGHEST BUILDING?

Something for you to argue about when you're marooned in a mountain hut. It's raining and there's nothing to read, not even a railway timetable. Where's the highest building in England? Not the tallest building – that's probably the Post Office Tower in London – but the building that's situated higher than anywhere else. It's probably in the Lake District, since the mountains there are the highest in England, but exactly where? You might say it's the huge cairn, about 9 feet high, on the summit of Scafell Pike (3,210 feet), for you can't get any higher in this country, south of the Border and excluding Wales, but perhaps you can't call this a building, although from afar the crumbling edifice looks like an hotel to some people, or so I'm told.

According to Wainwright, the guidebook writer who knew more about the hills of Lakeland than most people, 'the highest site ever used for building in England' was the so-called Smugglers' Hut, now completely disappeared, near the top of Central Gully on Gable Crag. This simple erection, which, even seventy years ago, I remember as little more than a few stones, perhaps a foot or so high, he infers was, at one time, the highest situated building in England. I estimate its height above sea level, although there's nothing to see there now, not even a couple of stones, at about 2,800 feet.

But there's another building near the top of another Lake District mountain, also at some 2,800 feet, that's still there to this day. This is the stone hut on Bowfell, and very few people indeed have even heard about it. In fact, the only person I've ever met who knows about this hut is Peter Fleming of Barrow-in-Furness, a fellow member of the Fell and Rock Climbing Club who, besides being an authority on the goosebields of Lakeland and other quirky things, happens to have climbed all the peaks in the Alps above 4,000 metres in height. Of course, Peter might have told other mountain friends about the hut.

I first stumbled on the Bowfell hut about fifty years ago while scrambling alone on the upper rocks of the mountain to the right or north of Bowfell Buttress. This is not a place for the ordinary walker, so don't go exploring there unless you're competent. It's a rough, craggy area and very exposed, with a big drop down to Mickleden. If you fell you would go a very long way and never go walking again. When you eventually find the hut – perhaps conducted there by a climbing friend – you will, at first, have difficulty in persuading yourself that it is, indeed, a stone hut, for it seems part and parcel of the crag. But then you might notice the big blocks of stone that form the roof.

Bowfell Buttress

After this first accidental discovery of the stone hut in the 1950s I promptly forgot its exact location and, in many visits to the area – once or twice when the crags were snowbound, making the search almost impossible – could not find it. Then, one day, perhaps about twenty years ago, I happened to mention the hut to Peter Fleming and discovered that he knew all about it.

'Yes,' he explained, 'it's still there. I was up there the other day.'

So, many years after my first discovery of the hut, I decided to go up there once again and try to pin it down. This time I went up the steep, craggy fellside from the sheepfold at the head of Mickleden to the foot of Bowfell Buttress. Traversing to the right I crossed the lower reaches of North Gully and then scrambled up the rough rocks of the craggy fellside – not as steep as Bowfell Buttress to its left but steep enough to a lone scrambler. When I reached the top of the rocks I began looking for the hut, for I remembered I had first found it in this area, and then spent the next hour or so in a futile search of likely places, even twice descending along a sort of shelf into North Gully. But all to no avail. The hut seemed to have disappeared.

Then, back on the shelf, I studied the crag in close detail, and suddenly, all at once, in a most unlikely place, there it was, straight in front of my nose. I think it was the big, square blocks of stone forming the roof that gave it away. Very soon I was inside, but I had first to take off my rucksack and go in backwards to effect an entrance. The Bowfell hut is hardly commodious: there's barely room for one person, but it would still provide welcome shelter in a storm or blizzard. Perhaps some shepherd had built it a hundred, two hundred years ago, as a shelter if overtaken by bad weather or darkness. But this craggy area, devoid of grass, seems an unlikely pasturage, even for Herdwicks, and hardly shepherd country. Perhaps, although I think it unlikely, it was some sort of look-out, for the views from this eyrie are widespread and spectacular. But who would want a look-out on the top of Bowfell? Smugglers? I hardly think so.

The better known former high building, because it's mentioned in several books and the Bowfell Hut is mentioned in only one of my own books, is the so-called Smugglers' Hut on Gable Crag, now completely disappeared, is similarly difficult to authenticate. Was it used by Moses Rigg, the legendary Honister quarryman turned whisky distiller and smuggler – he of the well-known Moses' Trod – and, if so, was it a store for whisky or wadd (plumbago from the Borrowdale mine) or even a look-out post or shelter? Many authorities have discounted all these theories. The place, they thought, was far too precariously perched to be accessible to nineteenth-century dalesmen. But the late George D. Abraham of Keswick, the distinguished pioneer climber and photographer who died in 1965 at the age of ninety-three, did not agree. He once told me that he was quite sure that Moses had actually had a still on that wild ledge on Gable Crag. Towards the end of the previous century, the nineteenth, the hut, he said, had had a roof, was stone-flagged and showed signs of having contained a still. Moreover, George Abraham explained to me, it was common talk in the dales at that time that this was where Moses made his brew from the bog water on Fleetwith Pike. Indeed, George said he had known one Dan Tyson, who claimed to have worked with Moses.

All this was told me very seriously by Mr Abraham, whom I knew quite well and who had often told me memories of his earlier days. Once I had spent the whole of a day in his Keswick home listening to him recalling great climbing days with, among others, Owen Glynne Jones, whom he considered the finest climber he had known. Even in his nineties George was alert, bright and vigorous with his memory quite unimpaired. For example, he recalled for me the details of a climb on Walla Crag he had first done in the 1890s that I happened to have climbed the previous day. Was the old root still there, as a foothold, on the first pitch, he asked as we chatted about details of this modest route he had first discovered as a youth?

But, sadly, other evidence suggests that Moses Rigg was already a legend in the nineteenth century in the days of Auld Will Ritson of the Wastwater Inn, in spite of the claim of Ritson, a noted storyteller, that as a lad he had known him. So there I must leave the story of the Smugglers' Hut on Gable Crag – unfinished. But, I'm quite sure the highest sited building in England is the stone hut on Bowfell, because it's still there, while the one that used to be on Gable Crag has, long years ago, fallen down Central Gully.

STEEP GRASS

When we first started exploring the Wasdale crags in the late 1920s we thought the front of Kirk Fell, facing the inn, must be the steepest fellside in the Lake District. It always seemed a terrible slog going up, and running down it at the end of a hard day fairly rattled up your thighs. Truth to say, we only really bothered with Kirk Fell when we were finishing off the Mosedale Horseshoe. There was, we thought at the time, no climbing on Kirk Fell and climbing was our main interest – it was some years later before we discovered the delightful climbs on Boat Howe – and our knowledge of Kirk Fell was mostly confined to the steep slope down which you trotted at the end of the Horseshoe. If your legs are up to the pounding this is one of the most rewarding descents in Lakeland with the door to the bar of the inn in which you will soon be downing well-deserved, foaming pints of ale enticingly in view all the way down.

However, since those early days, I've had to revise my youthful opinion about steep fellsides, having found several steeper places – grass and scree slopes, that is, not craggy mountainsides – places you can walk, if not actually trot, down. One of the steepest grass slopes that I regularly used until late in my eighties is the descent from the south top of Mellbreak direct to Crummock Water, which needs care, particularly at the top. I've never tried to trot down it – it's far too steep and, clearly, very much steeper than Kirk Fell, which I've run down many times.

But I don't think any of these – and other back-breaking Lakeland descents – are anywhere near as steep as some of the grass slopes in the Howgill Fells regularly traversed by Rough Fell sheep on their 9 inch wide trods. Walkers in the Howgills don't usually go up or down these slopes, unless they've got themselves lost because of the complexity of the terrain. They walk along the ridges where the going is straightforward, but, now and again, they find themselves traversing them, perhaps across Bram Rigg Top or around Black Force, and realise, with perhaps a shudder, how frightfully steep they are. Far too steep for trotting down and difficult for most people even to walk down. And in wintertime you're glad you've got

Black Force and the ravine of Black Force

your ice axe and perhaps your crampons in case of a slip. How many sheep, I've sometimes wondered, have slipped off these little narrow tracks and tumbled and slid, perhaps hundreds of feet, down the snow and ice? But perhaps sheep, those wonderfully agile mountaineers, don't fall.

I've always had a fascination for steep descents, not especially rough, rocky ground nor the unpleasant stony rivers that pass for paths in the fells nowadays, but steep grass. They are a challenge to get down in good, competent style, either trotting or, if the slope is too steep for that, walking, probably in zigzags, carefully down. I think the fascination stems from early skiing days, more than half a century ago, when you had to learn, in descent, how to turn into the fall-line. It was some time before I could pluck up the courage to do this, but, once mastered, it seemed a wonderful experience, and you felt king of the hill.

You could get a similar feeling of complete control when descending steep scree runs, in those distant, happy days when there were such places in the Lake District. Dore Head screes, steeply down into Wasdale's Mosedale from the Yewbarrow–Red Pike ridge, always made an exhilarating finish to a climbing day on Pillar or the Mosedale Horseshoe if you were missing out Yewbarrow or needing a quick way back to Wasdale Head. Nowadays, like other former good scree runs, it's quite useless with all the scree worn away. It was a disappointing, tiring descent when I last tried it and is best avoided nowadays, although sixty years ago, we sought it out as a special treat.

Descending steep grass I subconsciously get into the skiing position – body well forward, at right angles to the slope, knees bent, weight on the heels, and shoulders and arms ready for the turns, and find myself trotting down easily in successive zigzags, as you would when skiing.

Josie, my mountain partner in old age – my old age, not her's – had a rather different attitude to the descent of hills. When I got to the day's last summit I reckoned the job's been done, or, at least, that the hard work was over and that all we had to do now was to trot down. But when Josie reached the summit, having ascended in good style, the hard work of the day was about to begin – getting down. She rarely enjoyed descents which, properly done, should be so pleasurable.

In wheezy old age – before my feet and legs finally cracked up – I found coming down far easier than going up. The day was over, so far as the hard work was concerned, when I reached the summit; the rest, by comparison, was easy. Josie, however – and many others – thought the opposite. The hard work, they say, starts at the summit. They don't like going 'downbank', as we say in the fell country, and take longer to descend a hill than to climb it.

Although I've always been fascinated by steep descents this captivation eventually led to my downfall – ruined toes and feet. When we were climbing on Dow Crag more than seventy years ago we always ran down the screes at the end of the day, leaping precisely from boulder to boulder, and then carried on trotting down the fellside, with not many stops, all the way to Torver or Coniston. And when the car or motorcycle was parked at Coniston or we were catching the train back to Barrow, we invariably ran, in our clinker-nailed boots, all the way down the steep hill to the railway station, finishing off, although exhausted, with a splendid flourish, rather like a stop-christy at the foot of a ski run. We didn't realise at the time that all this pounding – ramming our toes into the front of our boots – would, eventually ruin our feet but, in my case, it certainly did, according to several orthopaedic surgeons who have studied them.

EYES OF THE MOUNTAIN

As an old cragsman – I did my last rock climbs at seventy-eight after devoting sixty years, week in, week out, to the craft of cragsmanship – I have always considered crags to be the most striking and interesting features of mountains, the features that give mountains their character. A mountain that had no crags, I felt, was not as fine a mountain as one that was regularly visited by climbers for its rock. But, reconsidering the matter, I have decided that this was really only my feeling when I was thinking about or approaching the mountains or seeing them from afar. When I was walking among them, not particularly intent on climbing, I believe I had different priorities.

Indeed, looking back on a long lifetime of mountains, I am sure that one of the most thrilling moments when walking in the hills is to come upon a tarn, especially when it is unexpected. Suddenly, just in front of you, perhaps half-hidden in the rocks, is a splendid pool of water, reflecting the sky, almost as if the sky, in all its colours, had been brought down to your feet. I have heard of tarns described as the 'tears of the mountain', but my old friend William Heaton Cooper, the painter, accurately described them in his splendid, definitive work *The Tarns of Lakeland* as 'the eyes of the mountain', an inspired description.

Lakeland tarns come in all shapes and sizes – some large enough for sailing a yacht, others just pools among the rocks. The largest is Devoke Water in remote country and commanding impressive views of the high fells; the smallest one to possess a name is Foxes Tarn on Scafell some way below the ridge of Mickledore. All tarns are beautiful, but some of them are perfect jewels of beauty.

I have bathed in dozens of Lakeland tarns, swum in many of them, fished in a few and skated on several, and often a tarn has been the highlight of a mountain day. One sultry summer day many, many years ago, coming down from the tops, my brother Leslie and I decided on a swim in Easedale Tarn to cool off a little. Very wisely, we left our clothes inside our rucksacks, fearing, in the intense humidity, that a deluge could be imminent. And, sure enough, when we were out in the middle of the tarn the heavens suddenly opened and there was an enormous cloudburst. There was, of course, no reason to abandon our dip, so we carried on swimming for some time, through the very dramatic downpour. And when we'd had enough we swam back to our rucksacks, put on our boots and walked down to Grasmere – or, rather, the wood just above Grasmere – completely naked. There was nobody about in such weather – it was still sheeting down – and we wouldn't have cared if there had been. I've never used a bathing costume in any of my tarn bathing for I never owned one, although I might have had one as a schoolboy when I went to swimming baths. So we just quietly dressed in our dry clothes in the welcome shelter of the woods and then walked down into Grasmere for a drink and a meal.

Leslie was almost fanatical in his tarn and pool bathing, far more enthusiastic than myself. Whenever he saw a tarn or pool in the fells he wanted to get into it, even when the weather seemed unsuitable for bathing. It was not unusual for him to have three or four bathes, or even more, in the day. He tanned easily and, because he never seemed to use a shirt for much of the year, always kept his tan throughout the winter. But even Leslie's predilection for tarn and pool bathing wasn't in the same league as that of two Grasmere friends of mine, Colin Dodgson, the proprietor of the tea-garden and other ventures, and Timothy Tyson, the little old village cobbler. They set about the strange task, mostly in winter when they had more time, of bathing in every tarn in the Lake District and completed the job in November 1959. Their definition of a tarn, as distinct from a pool, was something in which you could swim, even if only for a stroke or two. And, when they had bathed in the last of their tarns, high on the shoulder of Esk Pike, in a shower of hail, they reckoned there were exactly 463 of them.

Colin was nearly fifty when they finished the job, but Tim, with his bristly, white moustache and wire-rimmed spectacles, was seventy-five and a grandfather. Bathing in tarns, however, was, by no means, the only achievement of this remarkable pair. They had also between them in winter climbed all the mountains in England, Scotland, Wales and Ireland, and Colin had been one of the first men to reach the summit of all the 543 Munros and tops in Scotland. Tim had also done all the Munros years before this became fashionable and the thing to try to do, and kept his mouth shut about it, but hadn't managed all the tops. After all, he'd only started peak bagging when he was nearly fifty.

Tim, who died in 1967 – the little village cobbler who knew more about mountains than almost anybody else – was very much a mountain philosopher. Once, when he was in his eighties, he told me: 'It's the simple things that matter – snowflakes floating down on a quiet day, harebells among the rocks overlooking a pool, the heather on the fellsides, the water ousel cheerily singing in the beck, no matter how bad the weather, or the buzzards soaring.' And I liked this off-the-cuff remark from the little old cobbler so much that I had it printed on the title page of my last book, *The Coniston Tigers*.

The Grasmere pair had their favourite tarns. Colin was particularly fond of Blind Tarn in the Coniston fells – one of my favourites, too – and Small Water, while Tim considered the finest to be Hard Tarn, Lambfoot Dub, Broadcrag Tarn, Low Water and Innominate Tarn, where Wainwright's ashes have their resting place.

My own favourites would include the Coniston tarns, Goat's Water, Levers Water, Low Water and Blind Tarn, since I know them better than any others, and, of course, Lanty Tarn, high above Glenridding, my beloved Josie's favourite. I had first pointed it out to her, across the valley, when we were once descending from St Sunday Crag – a tiny flash of blue among the Scots pines – and promised I would take her there the next day, which I did, and she immediately fell in love with the tarn, its situation on the way to Helvellyn, the shadows of the trees in the water, its story – used for its annual supplies of ice for the big house in the valley – and its delightful name. Indeed, Josie decided to call a Kendal flat she then owned Lanty's and had the name carved on an oak name-plate. Years later she also decided that this was where she would like to rest at the end of her days, so we took her ashes up there in 2003.

Other favourite tarns of mine would include the necklace of Glaramara tarns, notably the perfect little jewel that Heaton Cooper calls Lincoln Tarn, Lambfoot Dub in the Scafells, the summit tarn on Haystacks, set in its perfect rock basin, and perhaps the tiny tarn on Shelter Crags – a little higher than the well-known Three Tarns – completely enclosed in rock with splendid, open views all round. The coldest tarn in which I've bathed is Hard Tarn, on a rocky shelf high up in Ruthwaite Cove below the Helvellyn ridge. It was also probably my shortest bathe – about three seconds.

Mind you, in my active youth with the Coniston Tigers on Dow Crag, we had a tradition of bathing in Goat's Water or Coniston Water every weekend, no matter what the weather. You couldn't back out of it: it was a test of manhood. But you could hardly call this bathing, let alone swimming. On the coldest days, sometimes with

Innominate Tarn, Haystacks

snow around or even ice, it was the merest token dip: just in and out with an astonished, breathless gasp.

The first Lakeland tarn in which I bathed was Beacon Tarn in the Blawith Fells, south of Torver. I was thirteen or fourteen years of age and decided, for some reason, that I wanted to bathe in this tarn, which, at that time, I'd never even seen. Perhaps I was deranged, through studying for some school exam. So I cycled alone from our home in Barrow-in-Furness, nearly 20 miles away, to Water Yeat, walked to the tarn, had my bathe – without a costume, of course – and then climbed the fell, Tarn Beacon, above the tarn. And, from its summit, I had the most remarkable, close-up view of the hills that were to become when I started rock climbing a few years later the most important in my life – Dow Crag, Brown Pike and Coniston Old Man, all smiling in the sunlight.

Then I went back to the toe of Coniston Water and, from Nibthwaite, climbed the rough, steep fell behind it. And here, on the little summit, I built a cairn, about four or five feet high, the only cairn I have ever built in the hills. As I rode back home on my bicycle, first to Greenodd, I kept looking back at my cairn, clearly outlined against the sky. It remained there for a year or two but then either fell down because of my bad workmanship or was demolished by vandals, a popular occupation for some thoughtless people. But, driving recently in the area, I noticed a prominent cairn in about the same place and wondered whether it had been rebuilt, although I was too lazy – too old, really – to scramble up and check.

Heaton Cooper wrote in his *The Tarns of Lakeland* that his favourite tarn, 'at all times of the year and under any conditions', was Sprinkling Tarn, underneath Great End: 'The most completely satisfying of all the tarns of Lakeland.' He gives many reasons for this choice, but mainly, he said, it was the character and feel of the place that finally attracted him so strongly. His book includes eighty-seven drawings of Lakeland tarns and sixteen plates in full colour, with a wonderful painting of Sprinkling Tarn as the frontispiece. A very good choice, I think.

There's one tarn in the Lakeland fells that's known as Griffin's Tarn, but only to my old friends, Ted Stacey and the late Ivan Waller, because I was 'always going on about it'. This is the tarn on the Steel Fell ridge above Greenburn. It is about 300 feet long but without a name and, until about the late 1980s, not marked on any map. I felt so strongly about this that I wrote to the Ordnance Survey suggesting they should, at least, show it on the map even if they didn't give it a name, and sure enough, they later drew in its distinctive blue shape. But, perhaps the Ordnance Survey had also taken notice of Heaton Cooper's earlier reference in his tarns book in which he calls the very large pool Steel Fell Tarn. My suggested name, to the Ordnance Survey, had been Boundary Tarn, since it lies on the former boundary between Cumberland and Westmorland, but they took no notice of this.

Many years earlier, though, I had had some success with the Ordnance Survey when I managed to persuade them to change Ernest Crag in Deepdale to Erne Nest Crag, an erne being a young eagle. Presumably, eagles nested on this crag in earlier days, but in the last century they moved several valleys further east, although, sadly, little has been heard of them recently.

I'm afraid I can't close this chapter without crossing swords – or, at least, quietly fencing – with my old friend Heaton about the highest tarn in Lakeland. He wrote that this was Broadcrag Tarn on Scafell Pike at a height of 2,746 feet, but there's a higher tarn than this on the Long Top 'Crinkle' of Crinkle Crags, which is 40 feet higher at 2,786 feet. The only problem is whether or not this is really a tarn. It certainly looks like one, measuring about 50 feet by 40 feet, but its depth, according to my correspondent, Mr David Copestake of Sedbergh, is only about 12 inches of water with 15 inches of silt, perhaps not deep enough for swimming. Tim and Colin liked their swimming pools to be at least waist deep.

David Copestake, who did all the research into the matter and sent me a wonderful colour photograph of the tarn, with the Scafells dramatically in the background, had long been doubtful about Heaton Cooper's claim and discussed the matter with me. I knew the tarn well and might have paddled in it but I don't think I ever bathed there. Incidentally, Broadcrag Tarn has a maximum depth, according to Heaton, of only 3 feet, barely qualifying for Tim and Colin's swimming requirements. Of course, the old master, Alf Wainwright, shows the tiny Long Top tarn in his Crinkle Crags summit sketch, but there is no mention of it by the authority on Lakeland tarns, William Heaton Cooper, the centenary of whose birth took place in 2003.

LIST OF ILLUSTRATIONS

INDEX